An Account of the Musical Celebrations on St Cecilia's Day

in the Sixteenth, Seventeenth and Eighteenth Centuries

WILLIAM HENRY HUSK

CAMBRIDGE
UNIVERSITY PRESS

CAMBRIDGE
UNIVERSITY PRESS

University Printing House, Cambridge, CB2 8BS, United Kingdom

Cambridge University Press is part of the University of Cambridge.
It furthers the University's mission by disseminating knowledge in the pursuit of
education, learning and research at the highest international levels of excellence.

www.cambridge.org
Information on this title: www.cambridge.org/9781108080323

This edition first published 1857
This digitally printed version 2015

ISBN 978-1-108-08032-3 Paperback

CAMBRIDGE LIBRARY COLLECTION

Books of enduring scholarly value

Music

The systematic academic study of music gave rise to works of description, analysis and criticism, by composers and performers, philosophers and anthropologists, historians and teachers, and by a new kind of scholar - the musicologist. This series makes available a range of significant works encompassing all aspects of the developing discipline.

An Account of the Musical Celebrations on St Cecilia's Day in the Sixteenth, Seventeenth and Eighteenth Centuries

Cecilia, a martyr of the early Christian church, has traditionally been honoured as the patron saint of music. Precisely how that association arose remains uncertain, yet she has inspired many composers over the centuries, notably Henry Purcell and Benjamin Britten. A music scholar and contributor to the first edition of Grove's *Dictionary*, William Henry Husk (1814–87) joined the Sacred Harmonic Society in 1834 and served as its librarian from 1852. This captivating work, first published in 1857, was prompted by what Husk felt to be unaccountable neglect by music historians of an important aspect of musical life. His carefully researched summary traces the musical celebrations of Cecilia's feast day, 22 November, in Britain and Europe from 1571 to 1846. An appendix gives the texts of numerous odes written for St Cecilia's Day, including pieces by Dryden and Brady, set to music by Handel and Purcell respectively.

Cambridge University Press has long been a pioneer in the reissuing of out-of-print titles from its own backlist, producing digital reprints of books that are still sought after by scholars and students but could not be reprinted economically using traditional technology. The Cambridge Library Collection extends this activity to a wider range of books which are still of importance to researchers and professionals, either for the source material they contain, or as landmarks in the history of their academic discipline.

Drawing from the world-renowned collections in the Cambridge University Library and other partner libraries, and guided by the advice of experts in each subject area, Cambridge University Press is using state-of-the-art scanning machines in its own Printing House to capture the content of each book selected for inclusion. The files are processed to give a consistently clear, crisp image, and the books finished to the high quality standard for which the Press is recognised around the world. The latest print-on-demand technology ensures that the books will remain available indefinitely, and that orders for single or multiple copies can quickly be supplied.

The Cambridge Library Collection brings back to life books of enduring scholarly value (including out-of-copyright works originally issued by other publishers) across a wide range of disciplines in the humanities and social sciences and in science and technology.

MUSICAL CELEBRATIONS ON

ST. CECILIA'S DAY.

AN ACCOUNT OF THE

MUSICAL CELEBRATIONS ON
ST. CECILIA'S DAY

IN THE SIXTEENTH, SEVENTEENTH AND
EIGHTEENTH CENTURIES.

TO WHICH IS APPENDED A COLLECTION OF

ODES ON ST. CECILIA'S DAY.

BY WILLIAM HENRY HUSK,

LIBRARIAN TO THE SACRED HARMONIC
SOCIETY.

LONDON:

BELL AND DALDY, 186 FLEET STREET.

1857.

PREFACE.

HE celebrations, of which an account is given in the following pages, have, notwithstanding the interest attaching to them, and their importance when regarded with reference to their results, been strangely neglected by our musical historians; Sir John Hawkins having contented himself with a few cursory remarks relative to the celebrations held in London towards the close of the seventeenth century, whilst Dr. Burney has left the subject entirely unnoticed. It is true that Malone in his *Life of Dryden* has devoted some space to a notice of the London celebrations, but his account, being only incidentally introduced as illustrative of his principal subject, is necessarily incomplete.

It is hoped that this little work may serve in some degree to supply this deficient portion of musical history. In the compilation of it great pains have been taken, by consulting every known and accessible source of information, to insure as far as practicable, accuracy and completeness; the result being the placing before the reader much information which has either not before appeared in print in England, or is wholly unpublished. The Odes written for the festival, and which will probably be considered as not the least interesting portion of the work, appear for the first time in a collected form.

I have to acknowledge my obligations not only to many of my friends, but also to several gentlemen to whom I was previously unknown, for the kind and ready assistance afforded me in the prosecution of my researches and for the communication of much valuable information. I may especially mention the Rev. Dr. Bliss, Principal of St. Mary Hall, and the Rev. Dr. Bloxam, Fellow and Librarian of Magdalen College, Oxford ; Horatio Townsend, Esq., of Dublin, Mr. Bennett, Organist of Chichester Cathedral, and more particularly my friend, Dr. Rimbault, whose kindness in allowing me the use of his curious and valuable library, and constant and ready communication of anything within his knowledge fitted for my purpose, have been of the most material service to me in the course of my work.

W. H. HUSK.

CONTENTS.

CELEBRATIONS ON ST. CECILIA'S DAY.

CHAPTER I.

The Legend of St. Cecilia.—Her Martyrdom and Ca-nonization.—Esteemed the Patroness of Music.—Custom of celebrating her Festival by Musical Per-formances.

T. CECILIA, we are informed by the writers of the *Golden Legend** and other authors, was a young Roman lady of noble birth, who being educated in the Christian faith, resolved to dedicate herself entirely to the service of God, to which end she made a vow of perpetual vir-ginity. Her parents, notwithstanding, caused her to espouse Valerianus, a Roman noble and a Pagan. Imme-diately after the marriage ceremony, Cecilia acquainted

---

* The *Legenda Aurea*, or *Golden Legend*, is a collection of the lives, &c. of the Saints, which was compiled about the year 1290 by Jacques de Voragine, or, as he is frequently called, Jacobus Januensis, Archbishop of Genoa. A French translation, entitled *Légende dorée*, was made soon after 1300 by a monk named Jehan de Vignay, from which Caxton made his English version, *The Golden Legend*.

her husband of her vow, and also that she was nightly visited by an Angel. Valerianus, fearing a rival, desired to see the Angel, but was told by Cecilia that it was impossible unless he first became a Christian. Consenting thereto, he was directed by his spouse to the retreat in which Pope Urban I., to avoid the Pagan persecutions, dwelt concealed, and having found and conversed with that Pontiff, was by him baptized. On his return home, he saw, on entering his chamber, the Angel, in the form of a beautiful young man, standing conversing with Cecilia. The Angel bore in his hand two crowns of roses and lilies gathered in Paradise, one of which he gave to Cecilia and the other to her husband, and commending the latter's faith, promised him whatever boon he should ask. Valerianus desired nothing but that his brother Tiburtius might also be converted. Tiburtius soon afterwards entering the apartment and perceiving the fragrant odour proceeding from the crowns of roses and lilies, which were invisible to him, in astonishment, asked whence it arose,—the season of flowers having passed. Being told of his brother's conversion, and urged by him and Cecilia, he agreed to join the Christian fellowship, and forthwith received baptism at the hands of Urban.

Persecution was then raging against the Christians, and the brothers were seized and carried before Almachius, the prefect, who, on their refusal to sacrifice to Jupiter, sentenced them to suffer death by decapitation. During their imprisonment they converted Maximus, one of the prefect's officers, who had charge of them. The circumstances attending their deaths being afterwards related by Maximus, not only excited the compassion, but occasioned the conversion of many persons, which so incensed Almachius that he caused Maximus to be scourged to death.

Cecilia was subsequently brought before the prefect, and refusing to sacrifice to the heathen deities was condemned to be put to death in a dry bath; *i. e.* a closed bath with fire beneath. This cruel sentence was carried into immediate execution, but the intense heat, instead of destroying, seemed rather to refresh Cecilia. An executioner was therefore sent to dispatch her with the sword, who gave her three wounds, but without succeeding in severing the head from the body. In this state she lived for three days, praying and exhorting the people, and at the end of that time, gave up the ghost.

These events are generally said to have occurred at Rome about the year 229 under the Emperor Alexander Severus; though they are by some supposed to have occurred between the years 176 and 180, under Marcus Aurelius, and in Sicily.*

The house in which Cecilia resided was, at her request, consecrated by Urban as a church; or, according to others, a church was erected on its site. Mention is made of a council held by Pope Symmachus in the year 500, in the church of St. Cecilia at Rome. Bede, in his *Ecclesiastical History*, relates that in this church Vilbrord, an Englishman, was ordained Archbishop of

---

* Dr. Burney says that Fortunatus of Poictiers, the most ancient author who speaks of St. Cecilia, and who wrote at the end of the sixth century, states her to have died in Sicily. (*History of Music*, ii. 377.)

Friesland by Pope Sergius, in the year 696. The church having fallen to decay was rebuilt by Pope Paschal I., who, in 821, translated thither from the cemeteries in which they had previously been interred, the bodies of Cecilia, Valerianus, Tiburtius, and Maximus, as well as those of Popes Urban and Lucius. In 1599, this church was again repaired and magnificently embellished by Cardinal Paul Emilius Sfrondati, nephew of Pope Gregory XIV., when, by order of Pope Clement VIII., the body of St. Cecilia was exhumed and examined in the presence of several dignitaries of the church, one of whom, Cardinal Baronius, has given an account of the appearance of the body. The remains were reinterred in a sumptuously enriched shrine, in the presence of the Pope and clergy, and a vast concourse of persons from the neighbouring towns. A marble statue, representing the Saint lying dead, in the attitude in which her body was found, was executed by Stefano Maderno, a sculptor in the employ of Cardinal Sfrondati.* This church is called St. Cecilia in Trastavere, or beyond the Tiber, to distinguish it from other churches in Rome dedicated to her. " The little room containing her bath, in which she was murdered or martyred, is now a chapel. The rich frescoes with which it was decorated are in a state of utter ruin from age and damp ; but the machinery for heating the bath, the pipes, the stoves, yet remain."† The celebrated

---

* Engravings of this statue may be seen in Hawkins' *History of Music*, 1776 (vol. iv. p. 503), and in Mrs. Jameson's *Sacred and Legendary Art*, second edition, 1850, p. 348.

† Mrs. Jameson's *Sacred and Legendary Art*, 347, second edition.

Wolsey derived from this church his title of Cardinal of
St. Cecilia beyond the Tiber.

" The beautiful legend of St. Cecilia is one of the
most ancient handed down to us by the early Church.
The veneration paid to her can be traced back to the
third century, in which she is supposed to have lived ;
and there can be little doubt that the main incidents of
her life and martyrdom are founded in fact, though
mixed up with the usual amount of marvels, parables,
and precepts, poetry and allegory, not the less attractive
and profitable for edification in times when men listened
and believed with the undoubting faith of children."*
" Mabillon (*De Liturgia Gallicana*, p. 175) has proved
that the festival of this Saint was celebrated in France
before the time of Charlemagne [who was born in 743]
by a Gallican Missal which he has published, and which
must have been in use before the Gregorian chant was
received in that country."†   The festival of " St. Cecilia, Virgin and Martyr," and also that of " SS. Valerianus, Tiburtius, and Maximus, Martyrs," continued
to be observed in the English Church until the Reforma-
tion,‡ and the name of the former is still retained in the
Calendar.   In the Roman and Greek Churches both
festivals are yet celebrated, the former on the 22nd of
November and the latter on the 14th of April.

To St. Cecilia is attributed the patronage of Music
and Musicians.

---

* Mrs. Jameson's *Sacred and Legendary Art*, 345, 2nd edit.
† Burney's *History of Music*, ii. 377.
‡ See the *Sarum Missal.*

Alban Butler (*Lives of the Saints*) says, " St. Cecily
from her assiduity in singing the Divine praises (in
which, according to her Acts, she often joined instrumental music with vocal), is regarded as the Patroness
of Church music."

There is, moreover, a tradition that the Angel by
whom Cecilia was visited was attracted to earth by the
charms of her singing.

Neither the tradition, nor the ascription of the patronage of music, however, would appear to be of very great
antiquity ; indeed, it seems pretty clear that, for a long
period, the Saint's musical attainments formed a by no
means conspicuous feature in her history. The early
poets, who, we may suppose, would eagerly have seized
on an incident affording such excellent opportunities
for the embellishment of the tale, make but very slight
mention of Cecilia's musical skill. Chaucer, for instance, who has made her history the theme of the tale
of one of his Canterbury Pilgrims—the Second Nun—
has contented himself with a close adherence to the
Golden Legend, and confines his notice of music to the
following lines, descriptive of the demeanour of Cecilia
on her wedding day :—

> " Whil the organs made melodie
> To God alloon in herte thus sang sche ;
> ' O Lord, my soule, and eek my body gye
> Unwemmed, lest that I confounded be.' "

these lines being an almost literal translation of a
passage in the *Golden Legend*.*

---

* The original passage, very slightly varied, viz. " Cantan-
tibus organis, Cecilia Domino decantabat dicens, Fiat cor

It is also remarkable that, although very ancient pictorial representations of St. Cecilia exist, she is seldom shown with musical instruments, or surrounded by musical attributes previous to the commencement of the fifteenth century. The most celebrated picture in which she is represented so accompanied is that painted by Raffaelle for the church of San Giovanni in Monte, near Bologna, in which she is seen standing with a regal or small portable organ in her hands, surrounded by St. Paul, St. John, St. Mary Magdalen, and St. Augustine.

The legend of St. Cecilia is a theme which has frequently employed the pens of dramatic writers. In 1667, one E. M. (conjectured to have been Matthew Medbourne, an actor at the Duke's theatre,) published " a Christian tragedy," entitled, " St. Cecilie, or, the Converted Twins," which he dedicated to Queen Catherine, but which was never acted; and Malone relates (on the authority of Dr. Burney), that in the *Drammaturgia* of Leoni Allacci are recorded thirteen dramas, tragedies, and oratorios, of which St. Cecilia is the heroine. Some of these are, no doubt, of the class of " holy tragedies," which (according to Riccoboni*) continued to be represented in Italy " in churches upon the celebration of the festivals of the Saint who gave name to the church," until about the year 1660, the period to which Allacci's account is brought down.

The writer is in possession of a MS. Oratorio en-

---

meum immaculatum ut non confundar," is used as the first Antiphon in the Romish ritual for St. Cecilia's day. (See the *Antiphonarium Romanum.*)

   * *Account of the Theatres in Europe.*

titled " Il Martirio di Santa Cecilia," by Quirino Colombani (a composer unnoticed by any musical authority),
which is undated, but would appear to have been written
about the end of the seventeenth century; and in which
the legend is closely followed, and no allusion whatever
made to Cecilia's skill in the tuneful art; an omission
the more surprising since the tradition as to her extraordinary musical powers had long before existed, and a
musical production would seem to have been a most
fitting vehicle for the celebration of her musical knowledge.

But whatever doubt or obscurity may exist as to the
Saint's musical acquirements, or when or how the
patronage of music was first ascribed to her, it is certain
that a custom of celebrating her festival, or rather of
celebrating on that day the praise of music (of which
she was regarded as the impersonation) by musical
performances, has prevailed at different times in various
countries, and there is no reason to doubt that such
practice is of considerable antiquity.

The earliest celebration of this kind of which any information has been obtained was one of a mixed character, partly religious and partly secular, which was
instituted at Evreux, in France, in the year 1571; a
particular account of which will be found at a subsequent
page.

A century, however, elapsed after the foundation of
that festival before anything of the same kind was established in England; the first celebration in this country,
of which any record remains, having taken place in the
metropolis in 1683. Whether this was instituted in

direct imitation of some foreign prototype, or was the result of an increasing taste for music as a means of public entertainment cannot now be ascertained, although there are some reasons for supposing the former to have been the case. But under whatever circumstances it was called into existence, a high degree of interest must ever be attached to it as the first of a series of meetings affording the earliest instances in this country of the periodical assemblage of large numbers of musicians, and to which the different meetings, which have been held for so many years past in various parts of the country under the name of Musical Festivals, and which have had so beneficial an influence in promoting and preserving a taste for the highest kinds of music, undoubtedly owe their origin.

CHAPTER II.

Celebrations of St. Cecilia's Day in England.

London.

S already stated, the earliest recorded musical celebration on St. Cecilia's day in this country took place in London in 1683. There may, possibly, have been some kind of celebrations at an earlier date, since Henry Purcell, writing in 1683, describes St. Cecilia's day as being " commemorated yearly by all musicians," and " annually honour'd by a Public Feast * * * *as well in England* as in Foreign parts ;"—and the Second Book of " *Choice Ayres, Songs, and Dialogues*," published in 1679, contains a song composed by Pelham Humphrys (who died in 1674), which is described as " sung at a Musick Feast,"—the name by which the annual celebrations were commonly designated,—and the words of which refer apparently to some meeting of annual occurrence.* Sir John Hawkins indeed, in his

---

* The following are the words of this song :—

" A Song, sung at a Musick Feast.
Verse Solo.
" How well doth this Harmonious Meeting prove
A Feast of Musick is a Feast of Love,

History of Music, states that " the lovers of music
" residing in this metropolis had a solemn annual meet-
" ing at Stationers' Hall on the twenty-second day of
" November, the anniversary of the martyrdom of St.
" Cecilia, from the time of rebuilding that edifice after
" the fire of London." He, however, adduces no evidence in support of this assertion, and the Books of the
Stationers' Company contain no entries relative to the
meeting prior to 1684. Such earlier meetings, supposing them to have existed, must however have been
of very limited extent, and there can be no doubt but
that the meeting of 1683 was considered, and justly
so, the first regular celebration of St. Cecilia's day in
England.

The " Musick Feasts" then instituted appear to have
been established and carried on under the auspices of a
body of persons associated together, (whether for any
other purpose than these celebrations cannot be traced,)
under the name of " The Musical Society." The members of this Society annually appointed certain of their
body (some of them professors of music and others amateurs), as stewards of the festival, to whom appears to
have been committed the task of making the requisite
arrangements. On the twenty-second day of Novem-

Where Kindness is our Tune, and we in parts
Do but sing forth the consorts of our hearts.
For friendship is nothing but concord of votes,
And Musick is made by a friendship of notes.
            Chorus. Three voices.
Come then to the God of our Art let us quaff,
For he once a year is reputed to laugh."

ber, the members of the Society attended Divine Service
at St. Bride's Church, where a choral service and an
anthem, occasionally composed for the festival, were
performed, and a sermon, usually in defence of church
music, was preached. They afterwards repaired to another place, where an ode in praise of music, written
and composed expressly for the festival, was performed;
after which they sat down to an entertainment.* The
vocal performers on these occasions appear to have consisted of the united choirs of St. Paul's Cathedral,
Westminster Abbey, and the Chapel-royal, together
with some of the singers attached to the theatres. No
female vocalists seem to have been employed, the treble
parts being supported by boys. The instrumentalists
probably comprised the members of the King's band
and of the theatrical orchestras. The number of persons engaged in the performance can only be conjectured;—the three choirs would probably afford about
thirty boys, and the adult singers, when allowance is
made for those who held appointments in more than one
choir, would perhaps number as many more. The band
might possibly consist of about twenty or twenty-five
persons.†

---

* It seems doubtful whether the custom of attending Divine
Service prevailed during the first ten years after the institution
of the festival. The account of the festivals published in 1692
[see page 26] mentions only the meeting for the performance of
the ode, and no sermon has been found of an earlier date than
1693.

† Congreve, describing the performance, concert-wise, of his
masque, " *The Judgment of Paris,*" in 1701, says, " the num-

The particular circumstances of each successive annual celebration held in London from the year 1683 will now be recorded.

A. D. 1683.—For this year's feast three odes were written, two in English and one in Latin, the music for all three being composed by Henry Purcell. It would seem, however, that only one of these was publicly performed. This was the production of Christopher Fishburn, a person of whom nothing is known, save that his name is attached (as the composer) to some songs in the fifth book of " *Choice Ayres, Songs, and Dialogues,*" 1684; and (sometimes as composer and at others as author) to several of the songs contained in D'Urfey's " *Wit and Mirth.*"* The place of performance has not been recorded, but it is most likely that it was the Concert Room in Villiers Street, York Buildings; then, and for many years afterwards, the principal place in the metropolis for public musical entertainments.† The

---

" ber of performers, besides the verse singers, was eighty-
" five :" and he seems to imply that such was, even then, an
unusual number.

* A Mr. Fishbourne is mentioned by Langbaine, Gildon,
and Jacob, and in the various editions of the *Biographia
Dramatica*, as the author of a play which was attempted to be
passed off as the production of the Earl of Rochester. He is
described as a gentleman of Gray's Inn, and was most likely
the same as the abovementioned person.

† This room was built and opened about 1680. Sir John
Hawkins (*History of Music*, 1776, v. 4,) says that the house
of which it was part was situated " on the right hand side of the
" street, near the bottom, and adjoining to what is now called
" the Water Office, but within these few years it was pulled

success of the performance seems to have equalled, if
not exceeded the expectations of the promoters of the
undertaking, who, encouraged by the result, immediately appointed four Stewards to conduct a similar
celebration in the following year; and those gentlemen
at once took active measures to ensure for the meeting
an at least equal success. The ode which had been
performed was published by the composer in the course
of the year 1684, with the following title and dedication:—" A Musical Entertainment, perform'd on
" November xxii, 1683, it being the Festival of St.
" Cecilia, a great Patroness of Music ; whose Memory
" is Annually honour'd by a public Feast made on that
" day by the Masters and Lovers of Music, as well in
" England as in Foreign parts." [Group of musical
instruments and books, surrounded by the motto, " Mu-
sica lætificat cor."] " London, Printed by J. Playford,
" Junior, and are to be sold by John Playford near the
" Temple Church and John Carr at the Middle Temple
" Gate, 1684."—" To the Gentlemen of the Musical
" Society, and particularly the Stewards for the year
" ensuing ; William Bridgman, Esq. Nicholas Stag-
" gins, Doctor in Music ; Gilbert Dolben, Esq. and Mr.
" Francis Forcer.* Gentlemen, Your kind Approba-

" down, and two small houses have been built on the site of
" it." The site is now believed to be occupied by a portion
of Hungerford Market.

  * William Bridgman was Secretary to the Ecclesiastical
Commission appointed by James II. in 1686, and also Clerk
of the Privy Council. He was examined as a witness for the
Crown on the trial of the Seven Bishops. He was also one of

" tion and benignant Reception of the performance of
" these musical compositions on St. Cecilia's day, by
" way of Gratitude demand this Dedication; which
" likewise furnishes the Author with an opportunity of
" letting the World know the Obligation he lies under
" to you; and that he is to all Lovers of Music, A real
" Friend and Servant, Henry Purcell." This ode is a

---

the Justices before whom Count Königsmark's accomplices
in the murder of Thynne were examined, and appeared in
company with Sir John Reresby (the other Justice) at the
trial, and produced the depositions taken on the examination.
He was well known as a dilettante musician, and is mentioned
by Roger North as one of the patrons of Nicola Matteis.

Dr. Nicholas Staggins held the appointment of composer to
Charles II. and subsequently that of Master of the Band of
Music to William III. In 1684 he was appointed Professor
of Music in the University of Cambridge, being the first who
held that office. He died in 1705. Several of his songs may
be found in the publications of the period, and in his official
capacity he composed some birth-day odes, but his abilities
were of a very inferior order.

Gilbert Dolben was the eldest son of Dr. John Dolben,
successively Bishop of Rochester and Archbishop of York.
He was appointed by William III. Justice of the Common
Pleas in Ireland, which office he held for twenty years. In
the reign of Queen Anne he was created a Baronet. His son,
Sir John Dolben, Prebendary of Durham and Sub-Dean of
the Chapel-royal, was also an amateur of music, and was intimately connected with Dr. Croft.

Francis Forcer was a musician by profession, and the composer of many songs printed in the *Theatre of Music.* Upon
the death of Sadler he became the proprietor of the Wells and
Music-house near Islington, the site of which is now occupied
by the theatre still bearing the name of Sadler's Wells, in
which he was succeeded by his son, who was the first that
introduced there the diversions of rope-dancing, tumbling, &c.

short composition* for solo voices and chorus, with accompaniments for stringed instruments only.   One of
the solos, " Here the Deities approve," was afterwards
printed in the collection of the composer's songs published by his widow, and entitled " Orpheus Britannicus."   The other two odes were never published.   That
in English (which probably was also the production of
Fishburn) is a composition of a similar description to
the printed one, except that neither counter-tenor voices
nor violas are employed in it.   A copy of this ode, in
the handwriting of the Rev. J. W. Dodd, formerly
under-master of Westminster School, is now in the
library of Dr. Rimbault.   The Latin ode, which in
character resembles a motet, is for three men's voices,
with accompaniments for two violins and bass.   A copy
of it, transcribed from the composer's original manuscript by Dr. Philip Hayes, is preserved in the library
of the Sacred Harmonic Society.   It bears the title of
" A Latin Song in honour of St. Cecilia, whose day is
" commemorated yearly by all musicians."

A. D. 1684.—The choice of a poet for 1684 fell upon
John Oldham, who produced an ode, the performance
of which, however, he was not destined to witness.   He
had but just completed his work when that scourge of
the period, the small-pox, laid him in an early grave.
He died on the ninth of December, 1683, aged thirty.†

---

* The complete score occupies only forty small quarto
pages.
† Oldham was the son of a Nonconformist Divine. He
took the degree of B. A. at Oxford in 1674, and subsequently

The task of setting Oldham's poem to music was assigned to Dr. John Blow, who, as we learn from the following announcement (which appears under the table of contents of the first book of the *Theatre of Music*) committed his composition to the press prior to its being performed : in doing which he was probably influenced by the success attending the publication of Purcell's ode for the preceding year.   " Advertisement.
" There is now in the Press a most excellent Musical
" Entertainment to be performed at the Musical Feast
" on St. Cecilia's day next, Nov. 22, 1684.   The
" words made by the late ingenious Mr. John Oldham,
" Author of the Satyr on the Jesuits, and other excel-
" lent Poems ; and set to Music in two, three, four, and
" five parts, by Dr. John Blow, Master of the Children,
" and one of the Organists of His Majesty's Chappel
" Royal.   Likewise at John Carr's Shop may be had,
" the Musical Entertainment for last St. Cecilia's day.
" The words made by Mr. Christopher Fishburn, and
" set to Music in two, three, four and six Parts, by Mr.
" Henry Purcell, Composer in Ordinary to His Sacred
" Majesty, and one of the Organists of His Majesty's
" Chappel Royal."   Blow's ode is described on the

---

became successively Usher of Croydon Free School and Tutor in several private families. At the time of his death he was residing in the family of William, Earl of Kingston, at Holme Pierpoint, Notts. (See Wood's *Athenæ Oxoniensis.*) His works have been frequently reprinted. " A Pindarique Pas-
" toral Ode on the death of my worthy friend, Mr. John
" Oldham," will be found amongst Thomas Flatman's *Poems and Songs,* fourth edit. 1686.

title-page as " A Second Musical Entertainment, Per-
" form'd on St. Cecilia's day, November xxii, 1684 ;"
a very strong and almost conclusive testimony that the
celebration of the previous year was the first of its kind
in London. The ode is on the model of those composed
by Purcell for 1683, and, like them, is accompanied by
stringed instruments only. It extends to seventy-one
pages, small quarto, and is dedicated " To the present
" Stewards, William Bridgman, Esq. Dr. Nicholas
" Staggins, Gilbert Dolben, Esq. Mr. Francis Forcer,
" and to the rest of the Gentlemen of the Musical So-
" ciety." One of the songs, " Music's the cordial of a
troubled breast," is also printed in the collection of Dr.
Blow's songs, published by him under the title of *Amphion Anglicus*. This ode appears to have been as
favourably received as its predecessor, both continuing to
be announced on the back pages and other " spare cor-
ners" of Playford and Carr's publications for several
years. The Concert Room in York Buildings, having,
it is supposed, been found insufficient for the accommo-
dation of the numerous assemblage which crowded to the
performance in the year preceding, occasioned a removal
this year to Stationers' Hall, where the festivals continued to be held down to the year 1703. The sum
paid for the use of the Hall appears from the following
entry in the Account of the Warden of the Company
from 5th July, 1684, to 25th July, 1685, under the
head of " Feasts and Funerals."*

---

* This heading, " Feasts and Funerals," has reference to
the then existing custom of several of the City Companies
(particularly those of the Merchant-Tailors and Stationers)

" Received, the 25th of November, 1684,
" for the Musick Feast kept in the Hall 2 0 0."

A. D. 1685.—The success which had attended the
first two meetings was no doubt mainly attributable to

---

letting their Halls for such festive entertainments as are at
the present time held at the large taverns, but for which, at
the period in question, no tavern afforded sufficient accommo-
dation. The annual gatherings of the gentry and others,
natives of several of the English counties, resident in London,
commonly called "The County Feasts" (in the holding of
which the men of Dorsetshire, Gloucestershire, Hampshire,
Oxfordshire, Warwickshire, Wiltshire, Worcestershire, and
Yorkshire seem to have been the most prominent), were amongst
the principal of such entertainments. They were kept with
great solemnity, the company first attending Divine service
(usually in the church of St. Mary-le-Bow), and hearing a
sermon (generally preached by a native of the county), and
afterwards repairing to the Feast in the Hall. It was for one
of these occasions (in the year 1690) that Henry Purcell
composed for the Yorkshire gentry his famous ode in celebration of the Revolution and the part taken in it by the men
of Yorkshire, which is commonly known as " The Yorkshire
Feast Song ;"—a production which D'Urfey (the author of
the words) justly calls " one of the finest compositions he ever
made," and which he tells us " cost £100 the performing :"
—a statement which throws some light on the probable expense of the performance of the Cecilian odes. The " Funerals" for which the halls were used were those of persons
whose obsequies were attended by a great concourse of rela-
tives and friends. The halls were on these occasions hung
with black draperies, which were kept for the purpose, and
the corpse being conveyed there over night, was thence borne,
followed by its long train of mourners, to its final resting-
place. The custom of giving concerts at Stationers' Hall continued for upwards of half a century after the time when the
Cecilian feasts were first held there.

the novelty of such celebrations in this country.   But
the means adopted by the Stewards for carrying their
object into effect must nevertheless have contributed in
a very great degree to the bringing about such a result.
Although the writer of the ode for 1683 was only an
obscure versifier, the composer chosen was one who not
only towered above all his contemporaries, but who is
regarded, even at this distance of time, as the greatest
musical genius our country ever produced ; one of whom
it has been truly said that he " is as much the pride of an
" Englishman in music, as Shakspeare in productions
" for the stage, Milton in epic poetry, Locke in meta-
" physics, or Sir Isaac Newton in philosophy and ma-
" thematics."*   Again ;—in 1684, a poet of at least
respectable ability was employed as the writer, whilst
the composer of the ode was second only to the illus-
trious individual who had been engaged the previous
year.   But the Stewards of 1685 were most unfortunate
in their selection of agents to carry on the festival ;
their choice resting upon persons by no means qualified
to support the reputation which the celebrations had
attained.   The commission to write the ode was given
to Nahum Tate, afterwards so well and unenviedly
known as the colleague of Dr. Brady in the concoction
of the collection of doggrel rhymes called the New
Version of the Psalms of David ; a production which
(as was said by Warton of the former version by Stern-
hold and Hopkins), " to the disgrace of sacred music,
" sacred poetry, and our established worship, still conti-

---

* Burney's *History of Music*, iii. 485.

" nues to be sung in the church of England ;"* and by his flippant and frivolous alterations of Shakspere's King Lear,—a monstrosity now happily banished from the stage. The labour of setting to music the precious specimen of " poetry" which Mr. Tate produced was imposed upon William Turner,† a composer of moderate abilities, who, it is perhaps not assuming too much to suppose, found himself (unlike Purcell, who could cover Fishburn's dross with his own refined gold,) unable to make anything of such worthless materials. His music has not been found, and has probably long since perished. Tate's lines were printed on a half sheet of paper, apparently for gratuitous distribution amongst the audience.

A. D. 1686.—The result of the festival of 1685 was evidently disastrous, and appears to have perilled the very existence of the meetings, since no performance took place in the following year.

A. D. 1687.—In 1687, however, the meeting was resumed, and the Stewards, determining to avoid, if

---

* *History of English Poetry,* iii. 461, edit. 1824.

† Turner was a member of the choirs of St. Paul's Cathedral, Westminster Abbey, and the Chapel-royal, and was chiefly celebrated as possessing a remarkably fine high counter-tenor voice. As a composer he contributed to the stores of our cathedral music, and also to the numerous collections of songs of his day. One of his anthems is contained in Dr. Boyce's Collection of Cathedral Music, and others are extant in manuscript. He died in 1740, at the very advanced age of eighty-eight, having survived his wife, to whom he had been married for nearly seventy years, only four days.

possible, the fate of their predecessors, took the most
energetic measures for promoting its success. They
sought and obtained the assistance of Dryden, and that
great poet, then in the zenith of his powers, produced
for them the fine ode commencing " From harmony,
from heav'nly harmony," undoubtedly (with the single
exception of its author's " Alexander's Feast,") the noblest lyric in the English language.* The composer
to whom this poem was entrusted was Giovanni Baptista
Draghi, an Italian musician who had settled in this
country, and who then held the appointment of organist
to Catherine of Braganza, the widow of Charles II.
He was an excellent composer, and, during a long
residence in England, had carefully studied the works
of the English composers, to whose style he had assi-
milated his own.† A copy of Draghi's composition,

---

* " This and the ode to the memory of Mrs. Anne Kille-
" grew, a performance much in the manner of Cowley, and
" which has been admired perhaps fully as much as it merits,
" were the only pieces of general poetry which he produced
" between the accession of James and the Revolution."
(Scott's *Life of Dryden*, edit. 1834, p. 293.)

† Draghi was a distinguished harpsichord player and music-
master to Queen Anne, and probably also to Queen Mary. He
composed much for the theatre. Pepys, in his *Diary*, under
date of 12th Feb., 1667, mentions having heard him (at Lord
Brouncker's house) sing through an act of an Italian opera
which he had written and composed at the instance of Thomas
Killegrew, who had an intention of occasionally introducing
such entertainments at the theatres. " I confess," says Pepys,
" I was mightily pleased with the musique." It is not known
whether this opera was ever produced. Draghi, however,
survived to witness the introduction into this country of the
Italian opera at the beginning of the next century. One of

which there are some reasons for believing to be in his autograph, is now preserved amongst the manuscripts in the library of the Sacred Harmonic Society. Besides minute directions as to the manner, &c. of performance, this copy furnishes us with the names of the principal vocalists employed in the execution of the work. These were the following :—Mr. Turner, Mr. Abell, Mr. Boucher, and Mr. Robart, counter-tenors ; Mr. Marsh, Mr. Church, and Mr. Freeman, tenors ; and Mr. Gosling, Mr. Woodson, Mr. James Hart, Mr. Bowman, and Mr. Williams, basses.* The principal

---

the latest pieces produced by him was an English opera called "The Wonders in the Sun," performed at the Queen's Theatre in the Haymarket in 1706.

* John Abell was one of the gentlemen of the Chapel-royal to Charles II. He was celebrated for his fine counter-tenor voice and for his skill as a lutenist. The king sent him to Italy, in order to show the Italians what good voices were produced in England. He returned from thence in 1682, and continued in the Chapel until the Revolution, when he was dismissed as a Papist. On this he again went abroad, and travelled through Holland and Germany to Poland. He continued absent until about 1700, when he came back to England, where he resided during the rest of his life.

Boucher (or Bouchier) was likewise a gentleman of the Chapel and also a singer at the theatre. The following curious paragraph relating to him appears in the *Flying Post*, August 16-18, 1696. "Mr. Boucher, a player, having for-"merly won 36,000 pistols from the Elector of Bavaria, who "promised to pay him at a convenient time, his Highness "hath now sent for him to come and take his money, and we "hear he goes accordingly with this convoy."

Robart's name occurs frequently as a singer in the Birth-day and New-year odes and at the concerts of the period.

Alphonsus Marsh, John Church, John Freeman, John Gos-

trebles are described as "ye boys." In this composition Draghi improved upon the orchestration of his predecessors by the addition to his score of wind instruments; trumpets and flutes being introduced in some movements of the ode. Dryden's poem was printed on a broadside with the title of " A Song for St. Cecilia's " day, 1687, written by John Dryden, Esq : and " compos'd by Mr. John Baptist Draghi ; " and the imprint, " Printed for T. Dring in Fleet Street, " 1687."

A. D. 1688.—The laudable exertions of the Stewards in 1687 for the restoration of the festival to its former

---

ling (or Gostling), Leonard Woodson, James Hart, and Daniel Williams, were all gentlemen of the Chapel-royal. Marsh, Church, and Hart were also composers of inferior note. Church (who was Master of the children, as well as gentleman of the Chapel) and Freeman also sang at the theatre. Gosling was famous for his deep bass voice, for the display of which many of Purcell's verse anthems are said to have been written; in Draghi's ode the part which he sang descends more than once to CC. Williams was also Clerk of the Cheque at the Chapel-royal.

John Bowman (born in 1666) was an actor and singer at the theatre. About 1673 he sang at the Duke's Theatre, and in 1680, sang a man's part in Lee's tragedy of " Theodosius." He married Elizabeth, daughter of Sir Francis Watson, Bart., who is described in the *History of the English Stage*, published by Curll, as " a very pretty player, both in her person and performances." Bowman died on 23rd March, 1739, aged eighty-eight, having acted on the previous 31st October, if not later. (Genest's *Account of the English Stage*, III., 581.) He was the original representative of Grimbald in Dryden and Purcell's " King Arthur," and Cardenio in " Don Quixote."

position were not, however, destined to meet with more
than a transient success. Other, and more important,
events than musical celebrations engaged the public
attention during the following year, and when St. Cecilia's day arrived, the Revolution was in full career;
William III. having landed at Torbay only eighteen
days before. During a period of such excitement, it
would, of course, have been useless to have held a
meeting, and it will therefore occasion no surprise to
find that there is, this year, nothing to record.*

A. D. 1689.—Nor was the next year more fortunate.
The public had doubtless not sufficiently recovered from
the effects of the great change which had so recently
occurred to justify the promoters of the " Musick feast "
in hazarding another meeting.

A. D. 1690.—The celebrations were, however, revived
in the ensuing year, when the ode was written by Thomas Shadwell, (who on the removal of Dryden had been
appointed poet-laureat,) and composed by Robert King,
a popular song-writer, whose compositions are to be
found in abundance in all the collections of the time.†
The poem is extant, but the music cannot be found.

---

* The expectation of William's arrival appears to have
diverted attention from public amusements for some time previously. Even the inauguration of the Lord Mayor on the
preceding 29th October, was stripped of its great attraction;
the customary pageants being omitted. (See Fairholt's *History of Lord Mayors' Pageants.*)

† He composed in 1693 an ode written by Peter Motteux
on the birthday of John Cecil, Earl of Exeter. In 1696 he

A. D. 1691.—St. Cecilia's day this year falling on a Sunday, the celebration took place on Monday, 23rd November. The ode was the production of the well-known Tom D'Urfey, and the music to it was supplied by Dr. Blow, whose talents were for the second time called into requisition to celebrate the praise of his art. No complete copy of the music has been met with, but two fragments, viz., a duet, " Couch'd by the pleasant " Heliconian spring," and a song, " Ah heav'n ! what " is't I hear," are printed in the composer's *Amphion Anglicus*. An interesting contemporary account of the celebrations now occurs. It is contained in the first number of the *Gentleman's Journal*, (a magazine edited and principally written by Peter Motteux,) published in January, 1691-2, and is as follows:—" The 22d of " November being St. Cecilia's day is observed through " all Europe by the lovers of music. In Italy, Ger- " many, France, and other countries, prizes are distri- " buted on that day, in some of the most considerable " towns, to such as make the best anthem in her praise. " She was a Roman lady of the noble family of the " Cœcilii, from whence the Cecils in England are said " to be descended. She is recorded to have been a lady " of an eminent beauty and piety and a lover of music, " having suffered martyrdom for the Christian faith, " for which she hath a place allowed her by the Church " of Rome in the Calendar. If you will believe their " legends, she had espoused a fine gentleman and lived

took the degree of Bachelor of Music in the University of Cambridge. A collection of twenty-four of his songs was printed by the elder Walsh.

" with him till his death, yet remained a Virgin ; and
" refusing to sacrifice to the Gods, was shut up in one of
" the baths in her own house being empty and without
" water ; and tho' a great fire was made under it for
" a day and night, yet far from receiving hurt by it, it
" seemed to her a place of pleasure and refreshing, which
" one Almachius seeing, he ordered her head to be cut
" off in that place. They add, that the hangman gave
" her three blows, yet did not cut off her head altoge-
" ther, but left it even as it was hanging by the skin,
" and that she lived three days thus wounded, comfort-
" ing those that came to see her. This Alfonso Vil-
" legas, a Spanish compiler of legends, whose book is
" printed with an approbation of the Divines of Doway,
" relates. Tho' the last of these miracles must seem
" but small to those that have read of St. Denys carry-
" ing his head in his hand three or four miles, or St.
" Patrick's swimming with his in his teeth ; that about
" her husband will doubtless be called in question. On
" that day or the next, when it falls on a Sunday, as it
" did last time, most of the lovers of music, whereof
" many are persons of the first rank, meet at Stationers'
" Hall in London, not thro' a principle of supersti-
" tion, but to propagate the advancement of that divine
" science. A splendid entertainment is provided, and
" before it is always a performance of music by the best
" voices and hands in town ; the words, which are
" always in the patronesses praise, are set by some of
" the greatest masters in town. This year, Dr. John
" Blow, that famous musician, composed the music ;
" and Mr. D'Urfey, whose skill in things of that nature

" is well enough known, made the words. Six Stew-
" ards are chosen for each ensuing year; four of whom
" are either persons of quality or gentlemen of note,
" and the two last either gentlemen of their Majesties'
" music, or some of the chief masters in town. Those
" for last year were, the Honourable James Saunder-
" son, Esq. ; Sir Frances Head, Baronet ; Sir Thomas
" Samwell, Baronet ; Charles Blunt, Esq. ; Mr. John
" Goodwin, and Mr. Robert Carr ; and those chosen for
" the next, Sir Thomas Travel, Bar ; Josias Ent,
" Esq. ; Sir Charles Carteret, Bar ; John Jeffrys,
" Esq. ; Henry Hazard, Esq., and Mr. Barkhurst.*
" This feast is one of the genteelest in the world ; there
" are no formalities nor gatherings, like as at others,
" and the appearance there is always very splendid.
" Whilst the company is at table, the hautboys and
" trumpets play successively. Mr. Showers † hath
" taught the latter of late years to sound with all the
" softness imaginable ; they plaid us some flat tunes

---

* Robert Carr, John Goodwin and Barkhurst were professors of music.

† This was John Shore, son of Matthias Shore, the Serjeant Trumpeter, and the most celebrated trumpet player of
his time. He is said to have been an especial favourite of
Purcell, who frequently wrote solo parts for the trumpet expressly for Shore to play. One of the pieces so accompanied
was the song, " Genius of England," which was sung by
Shore's sister, Mrs. Cibber. John Shore became Serjeant
Trumpeter on the death of his uncle, William, who had succeeded Matthias Shore in that place. On John Shore's death
in 1753, Valentine Snow, an equally famous performer, for
whom Handel wrote the difficult solo parts for the trumpet in
his oratorios, &c., was appointed his successor in office.

" made by Mr. Finger with a general applause, it
" being a thing formerly thought impossible upon an
" instrument designed for a sharp key."

A.D. 1692.—In 1692, Nicholas Brady, then minister
of St. Catherine Cree Church, and lecturer of St. Michael's, Wood Street, and also chaplain to the king
and queen—the fellow-labourer of Tate in the manu-
facture of the new version of the Psalms—furnished an
ode, which had the good fortune to be set to music by
Henry Purcell. This was undoubtedly, in a musical
point of view, the most successful production of the
entire series of Cecilian odes. Its popularity is attested
by the numerous manuscript scores still extant, as well
as by the insertion of several of the songs in the *Orpheus Britannicus*. It has been printed entire in our
own time by the Musical Antiquarian Society, being
the last work issued by that body. A manuscript score
in the library of Dr. Rimbault, who edited the ode for
the Musical Antiquarian Society, bearing the date of
1699, gives the names of the following singers as
engaged in its performance; viz. Mr. Turner, Mr.
Howell, Mr. Pate, Mr. Damascene, Mr. Snow, Mr.
Woodson, Mr. Bowman, and Mr. Williams.* These

---

* John Howell was a counter-tenor singer, and a member
of the choir of the Chapel-royal.

Pate was a singer at the theatres. The following paragraph, in which his name occurs, furnishes a curious illustra-
tion of the authority formerly exercised over the players
(" His Majesty's servants,") by the Lord Chamberlain. " I
" am informed that the Lord Chamberlain hath been pleased
" to displace Mr. Pate and Mr. Reading from their places in

gentlemen were not, however, the only vocalists, since we find from the *Gentleman's Journal* for November, 1692, that one of the solos was sung by Purcell himself. This interesting record, the only one existing, of the great composer's vocal performance, is as follows :—" In my first Journal I gave you a large account " of the Musick Feast on St. Cecilia's day ; So, to avoid " repetitions, I shall onely tell you that the last was no " ways inferiour to the former.   The stewards chosen " for the next year are, the Right Honourable the " Lord Kennedy ;   Norton, Esquire ; Sir John " Woodhouse, Baronet ; Phillip Wheak, Esquire ; Mr. " Godfrey Finger, and Mr. Bingham.   The following " Ode was admirably set to Music by Mr. Henry Pur- " cell, and performed twice with universal applause, " particularly the second Stanza, which was sung with " incredible graces by Mr. Purcell himself.*   Though " I was enjoined not to name the Authour of the Ode,

---

" the Playhouse for being in the late riot at Drury Lane." (*Post-Boy*, June 20th, 1695.) It appears by another news-paper (*The Flying Post*, July 6-9, 1695,) that the riot was at the Dog Tavern, and that several persons were prosecuted and found guilty, and fined as much as 500 marks each, and that Pate and Reading were fined only 20 marks each ; probably in consideration of the punishment of dismissal inflicted on them by the Chamberlain.   They appear, however, to have been soon after reinstated in their employment.

    Alexander Damascene and Moses Snow were gentlemen of the Chapel-royal.   Many of their songs are to be met with in the Collections of the day.   An anthem by Snow is printed in *The Divine Companion*, one of Playford's publications.

    * The counter-tenor solo, " 'Tis Nature's voice." The " incredible graces" may be seen in the score, where they are written out at length.

" I find a great deal of reluctancy to forbear letting
" you know whom you must thank for so beautifull a
" Poem ; and to use Ovid's words,—

" Se quoque nunc, quamvis est jussa quiescere, quinte
" Nominet invitum, vix mea Musa tenet."

Then follow the words of the ode. In January, 1693,
the ode is again referred to, in the same magazine, on
the insertion of an epigram by " Mr. B——y, whose
" Ode for St. Cecilia's day you liked so well." About
a year afterwards the ode is found announced for performance at a concert, in the following terms :—" At
" the Consort-room in York-buildings, on this present
" Thursday at the usual hour, will be performed Mr.
" Purcell's Song, composed for St. Cecilia's Day in
" the year 1692, together with some other composi-
" tions of his,* both vocal and instrumental, for the
" entertainment of his Highness Prince Lewis of
" Baden." (*London Gazette*, No. 2943, January 25,
1693.)

A.D. 1693.—The festival had now acquired great
importance and popularity, and had become an object
of such general interest as to induce the announcement
of it in the *London Gazette*, and we accordingly find
the following notification appearing in No. 2924 of
that publication, on Monday, November 20th, 1693.
" The Anniversary Feast of the Society of Gentlemen,

---

* One of these " other compositions" (a song entitled
" Sawney is a bonny lad,") may be found in the *Gentleman's
Journal* for January and February, 1694, and in the Second
Book of the Collection of Songs entitled " *Thesaurus Musicus.*"

" lovers of Musick, will be kept at Stationers' Hall on
" Wednesday, the 22nd inst. Tickets are delivered
" at Mr. Richard Hoare's, goldsmith, at the Golden
" Bottle in Fleet Street,* and at Mr. Jer. Marlow's,
" goldsmith, at the Spread Eagle in Lombard Street."
The ode this year was the production of Theophilus
Parsons, and was set to music by Godfrey Finger, one
of the Stewards of the previous year.† A sermon was
preached at St. Bride's church, (on Psalm c. 1, 2,)
by Dr. Ralph Battell, Sub-dean of the Chapel-royal,‡

---

* The descendants and successors of this gentleman still re-
tain the sign of the Golden Bottle over the door of their Bank-
ing-house in Fleet Street, and on the cheques issued by them.

† Gottfried (or Godfrey) Finger, a native of Olmutz in
Moravia, resided in England for many years. In 1685 he was
appointed Chapel-master to James II. He composed several
sets of Sonatas for violins and other instruments, as well as the
music for numerous dramatic pieces. In 1699, " several persons of quality" having, " for the encouragement of musick,"
raised a sum of two hundred guineas, to be distributed in four
prizes of one hundred, fifty, thirty and twenty guineas, " to
such masters as should be adjudged to compose the best,"
publicly invited a competition for the same. The poem chosen
for composition was Congreve's " *Judgment of Paris.*" Finger
entered the lists, and on the adjudication of the prizes was
awarded the fourth, the others being given to John Weldon,
John Eccles, and Daniel Purcell. He was so dissatisfied with
this decision and the reception his composition met with when
publicly performed, that he quitted England and returned to
Germany, where, in 1702, he obtained the appointment of
chamber-musician to Sophia Charlotte, Queen of Prussia, and
in 1717, that of chapel-master at Gotha.

‡ Dr. Battell was of Peter House, Cambridge. In 1662, he
succeeded Humphry Talbot as Rector of All Saints, with the
vicarage of St. John annexed, in the town of Hertford, and in
1680 (on the decease of Joseph Glanvill) was made a Prebend-

who asserted in it " the lawfulness and expediency of " Church Music," and in support of his arguments cited not only Scripture and the Fathers, but also Hooker, Baxter, and the Genevan divines. This sermon was printed in the December following at the request of the Stewards. The growing desire of hearing the odes subsequently to their original performance is evidenced by the following advertisements extracted from the *London Gazette* :—" In York Buildings, on Monday " next, will be performed the last St. Cecilia's Song, " beginning at the usual hour." (No. 2939, Thursday, January 11th, 1693-4.) " At the consort in York " buildings, on Monday next, the 5th instant, will be " performed Mr. Finger's St. Cecilia's Song, inter- " mixed with a variety of new musick at the ordinary " rates." (No. 2945, Thursday, February 1st, 1693-4.)

A.D. 1694.—The rent of Stationers' Hall, which for the past ten years had remained fixed at £2, was this year raised. An entry appears in one of the Company's books (F. 194 a.) of an order, that " in consideration " of the damage that may be done to the Hall at the " next Cecilia's Feast, by setting up scaffolding and " fixing tables and benches, the Hall shall not be let " for that occasion under £5." The " scaffolding " was no doubt the orchestra required for the performance of the ode. The Stewards, however, succeeded in pre- vailing upon the authorities not to enforce this order to

---

ary of Worcester. In 1689, he was appointed (on the resig- nation of Dr. William Holder) Sub-dean of the Chapel-royal, which he held until his death, March 20th, 1712-3.

its full extent, since we find that in this and each of the next two years, £4 only were paid as rent. It has not been discovered by whom the ode performed this year was written or composed. In the Fourth Book of the Collection of Songs, entitled " *Thesaurus Musicus*," (published in 1695,) there is a song entitled " Mr. Picket's Song, sung at St. Celia's Feast by Mr. " Robart," which may possibly be a portion of the ode for this year's festival, but who or what the composer, Picket, was, or how he came to be selected for such a purpose, is altogether unknown, as in no other place is the slightest notice of him to be met with. The church service this year was celebrated with unusual magnificence, Purcell having produced for the occasion his celebrated Te Deum and Jubilate in D. This fine composition met with so favourable a reception, and attracted such universal admiration, that the Society (as we learn from the dedicatory epistle prefixed to the score, when published by the composer's widow in 1697,) expressed an intention of having it repeated at their annual meeting. This intention was not, however, carried into immediate effect, the next year having witnessed the production of a Te Deum and Jubilate by Dr. Blow; but it seems highly probable that it was subsequently acted on. Of the popularity of Purcell's composition no further evidence is needed than is furnished by the fact, that it was constantly performed at the Festivals of the Sons of the Clergy in St. Paul's Cathedral, from the time when music was first made a prominent feature in those celebrations,* until the pro-

---

* The date of this event is very variously stated. Dr. Burney places it in 1695 : a palpable error, inasmuch as St.

duction of Handel's Te Deum and Jubilate, composed
on the Peace of Utrecht in 1713, and from that period
was performed alternately with Handel's composition
until 1743, when both were laid aside in favour of the
Te Deum produced by Handel on the occasion of the
victory at Dettingen. So completely, indeed, had Purcell's work become identified with these meetings, that the
occasion for which it was written seems to have been lost
sight of in the purpose to which it was afterwards applied; and in the frequent republications of it we find it
invariably described as " Te Deum et Jubilate for
" Voices and Instruments, perform'd before the Sons of
" the Clergy, at the Cathedral Church of St. Paul,
" composed by the late Mr. Henry Purcel." Nor was
the favour with which it was received confined to the
metropolis. At the provincial celebrations of St. Cecilia's day, and at the meetings of the three choirs of
Gloucester, Worcester, and Hereford, it continued in
constant use until displaced by the same composition
which superseded it in London.

A.D. 1695.—The cup of delight of which the votaries
of music had been wont to drink on St. Cecilia's day,
was this year mingled with sorrow. One whose strains

Paul's was not opened for service until 2nd December, 1697.
Sir John Hawkins states it to have been about 1697, in which
year the annual festivals were removed from Bow Church to
the Cathedral; whilst Mr. Lysons in his *History of the Meetings of the Three Choirs*, asserts positively that music was first
introduced in 1709. The unfortunate destruction by fire, in
1838, of the early records of the festival, has, it is feared, rendered the chance of arriving at a knowledge of the true date
exceedingly doubtful.

had so often raised them to ecstacy, whose genius had
cast so bright a light on their very last celebration, had
passed from amongst them. In the flower of his man-
hood and in the plenitude of his powers, Henry Purcell
had on the preceding day yielded up his spirit. The
assembly, we may readily conceive, wore an aspect of
sadness, albeit the occasion was one of rejoicing. The
Stewards of this year's feast were Lord Drummond,
Sir Thomas Murray, Bart., J. Crauford, Esq., James
Harris, Esq., Phil. Howard, Esq., Archibald Hutchin-
son, Esq., Ant. Robert, Gent., and John Bowman,
Gent.* The church service was this year again distinguished by the production of a grand Te Deum and
Jubilate; Dr. Blow being the composer on the present
occasion. From his original manuscript, which is still
existing, we learn that Messrs. Howell, Turner, Barnes,
Freeman, Church, Williams, Woodson, and Leveridge,†
were the singers to whom the execution of the verse
parts was entrusted. The sermon was preached by
Dr. Charles Hickman.‡ It is upon the first verse of

---

* James Harris was probably Harris of Salisbury, the father
of the author of *Hermes*, and grandfather of the first Earl of
Malmesbury. The professional Stewards, Robert (or Robart),
and Bowman, have been before noticed.

† Charles Barnes was a gentleman of the Chapel-royal.
His voice was a counter-tenor. Richard Leveridge was the
well-known theatrical singer, whose "deep and powerful
bass" voice delighted the public for many years afterwards.

‡ Dr. Hickman was a native of Northamptonshire, and a
son of William Hickman of Barnack in that county. In 1667,
being then about 18 years of age, he became a student of
Christ Church, Oxford. He afterwards held the Rectory of

the one hundredth Psalm, and consists principally of arguments and evidences in favour of the use of music in public worship. It was published, at the request of the Stewards, in 1696. No direct traces of any ode for this year are to be found. There is, however, extant (in the library of Dr. Rimbault,) a short ode by Dr. Blow, the words of which are suited to a " Musick feast," and which may possibly have been written for this year's celebration. That it was composed before 1700 is apparent from the circumstance of a selection from its solo parts and symphonies being worked up into a song, to form what the composer terms the " Prologue " to his " *Amphion Anglicus.*"

A. D. 1696.—The feast was this year advertised in the *London Gazette* to take place on Monday, the 23rd of November, " being the sequel of St. Cecilia's day," and the tickets were to be delivered at Mr. Richard Glover's, at the Castle Tavern in Fleet Street. The ode was composed by Nicola Matteis, a famous Italian violinist, who had settled in England, and was at this period greatly patronized.* Not only was he engaged

---

St. Ebbs in that city, and subsequently became chaplain to Charles, Duke of Southampton. In 1680 he was appointed chaplain to James, Lord Chandois, then going as ambassador to Constantinople, and in 1684 was made chaplain to the Lord Lieutenant of Ireland. In February, 1684-5, he took the degree of D.D. He was next appointed chaplain in ordinary to William and Mary, and in July, 1692, was made Lecturer of St. James, Westminster. He was also Rector of Hogsnorton, Leicestershire.

* Matteis came to England about the year 1674, at which period we find his performance on the violin recorded by Eve-

to compose the ode for the London celebration, but he
was also one of the Stewards for conducting a celebration at Oxford, at which place it seems likely that an
ode of his was also performed ; and as the Oxford
meeting was not held until the 27th November, it is possible that the ode there performed was that which had just
before been produced in London. Neither Matteis' music, nor the words of the ode, nor the name of the author
of the latter has been discovered. According to what
had now become a regular custom, the ode was announced for performance at a public concert soon after
its production. The advertisement runs thus :—" The
" musick that was performed of St. Cecilia's Day,
" composed by Signor Nicola, will be performed on
" Thursday night, in York-buildings, being the 7th
" instant." (*London Gazette*, No. 3250, Monday,
January 4th, 1696-7.)

A. D. 1697.—The rent of Stationers' Hall, which
for the past three years had been £4, was this time
increased to £5. The Stewards for conducting the
festival were Hugh Colvill, Esq. Captain Thomas
Newnam, Orlando Bridgman, Esq.* Theophilus Butler,

---

lyn. (See his *Diary*, November 19th and December 2nd, 1674.)
He published here several instrumental compositions, and
also a work on thorough bass. An interesting account of him
is given by the Hon. Roger North, in his *Memoires of Musicke*.
The time of his death is not known, but it was prior to 1728,
the year in which North wrote. The disorder of which he
died is said by North to have been occasioned by his having,
" *after the manner of his country*, lived luxuriously."
     * Grandson of Lord Keeper Bridgman.

Esq. Leonard Wessel, Esq. Paris Slaughter, Esq. Jeremiah Clarke, Gent. and Francis Le Riche, Gent. (the
two latter being the professional Stewards). For the
church service an anthem with instrumental symphonies, &c. ("The king shall rejoice,") was produced by
William Turner, the composer of the ode for 1685, who
in the preceding year had taken the degree of Doctor
in Music at Cambridge. A copy of this anthem is
preserved in the third volume of the Tudway Collection
of church music in the British Museum. (Harleian MS.
7339.)* Dr. Brady (the author of the ode for 1692)
preached a sermon on the text, ɪɪ Chronicles, chap. v.
verses 13 and 14. This was afterwards published with
the title of " Church Music vindicated." In the dedication to the Stewards, prefixed to it, the author alludes
to the musical portion of the church service, which he
describes as " that admirable performance, which, by
" a management peculiar to yourselves, laboured under
" no disadvantages of disorder or confusion." Purcell's
Te Deum and Jubilate, originally produced at the
festival of 1694, were probably repeated at this meeting. Those fine compositions had been published by
the author's widow, with the following title and dedication: " Te Deum & Jubilate, for Voices and In-
" struments, Made for St. Cecilia's Day, 1694. By the

---

* This composition appears to have been held in some re-
pute. It formed part of a " performance of Divine Musick,
" for the Entertainment of the Lords Spiritual & Temporal
" and the Honourable House of Commons, at Stationers' Hall,
" January the 31st. 1701. Undertaken by Cavendish Weedon,
" Esq."

" late Mr. Henry Purcell. London, Printed by J.
" Heptinstall for the Author's Widow; and are to be
" sold by Henry Playford, at his Shop in the Temple
" Change in Fleet Street, 1697."—" To the Right
" Reverend Father in God, Nathaniel [Crewe,] Lord
" Bishop of Durham.*   My Lord, The Ambition I
" have to do the greatest Honour I can to the Memory
" of my Dear Husband, by inscribing some of his best
" Compositions to the best Patrons both of the Science
" he profess'd and of his performances in it, is the fairest
" Apology I can make to your Lordship ; as it was the
" main Inducement to myself for placing your Lordship's
" Name before this Piece of Musick.   The Pains he be-
" stow'd in preparing it for so Great and Judicious an
" Auditory, were highly rewarded by their kind Recep-
" tion of it when it was first Perform'd ; and more yet
" by their Intention to have it repeated at their *Annual*
" *Meeting ;* but will receive the last and highest Honour
" by your Lordship's favourable Reception of it from
" the Press, to which I have committed it, that I might
" at once gratifie the Desires of several Gentlemen to
" see the Score, and at the same time give myself an
" Opportunity to acknowledge, in the most Publick and
" Gratefull Manner, the many Favours Your Lordship
" has bestow'd on my Deceased Husband, and conse-
" quently on Your Lordship's Most Oblig'd and most

---

* This prelate was throughout life a " lover of musick."
He is mentioned by Wood as one of those who attended the
weekly meetings at the house of Will. Ellis in Oxford in 1658.
According to honest Anthony, he was " a violinist and violist,
" but alwaies played out of tune, as having no good eare."

" Humble Servant, F. Purcell." Dryden, who was
applied to by the Stewards to furnish them with an ode,
produced for this festival his celebrated " Alexander's
Feast, or the Power of Musick." The poet, in a letter
to his son, written in September this year, thus relates
the manner of the application, and the reason which
induced his compliance. " I am writing," he says, " a
" song for St. Cecilia's feast; who, you know, is the
" patroness of Music. This is troublesome, and in no
" way beneficial; but I could not deny the stewards, who
" came in a body to my house to desire that kindness,
" one of them being Mr. Bridgeman, whose parents
" are your mother's friends." " This account," says
Sir Walter Scott, " seems to imply that the Ode was a
" work of some time; which is countenanced by Dr.
" Birch's expression, that Dryden himself ' observes
" in an original letter of his, that he was employed
" for almost a fortnight in composing and correcting
" it.' On the other hand, the following anecdote is told
" upon very respectable authority. ' Mr. St. John,
" afterwards Lord Bolingbroke, happening to pay a
" morning visit to Dryden, whom he always respected,
" found him in an unusual agitation of spirits, even to a
" trembling. On inquiring the cause; I have been up
" all night, replied the old bard; my musical friends
" made me promise to write them an Ode for their
" feast of St. Cecilia: I have been so struck with the
" subject that occurred to me, that I could not leave it
" until I had *completed* it; here it is, *finished* at one
" sitting.' And immediately he shewed him *this* Ode,
" which places the British lyric poetry far above that

" of every other nation.' These accounts are not,
" however, so contradictory as they may at first sight
" appear. It is possible that Dryden may have com-
" pleted at one sitting the whole Ode, and yet have
" employed a fortnight, or much more, in correction.
" There is strong internal evidence to show that the
" poem was, speaking with reference to its general
" structure, wrought off at once. A halt or pause,
" even of a day, would perhaps have injured that con-
" tinuous flow of poetical language and description,
" which argues the whole scene to have arisen at once
" upon the author's imagination. It seems possible,
" more especially in lyrical poetry, to discover where
" the author has paused for any length of time; for
" the union of the parts is rarely so perfect as not to
" show a different strain of thought and feeling. There
" may be something fanciful however in this reasoning,
" which I therefore abandon to the reader's mercy;
" only begging him to observe, that we have no mode
" of estimating the exertions of a quality so capricious
" as a poetic imagination; so that it is very possible
" that the Ode to St. Cecilia may have been the work
" of twenty-four hours, whilst corrections and emenda-
" tions, perhaps of no very great consequence, occupied
" the author as many days. Derrick, in his Life of
" Dryden, tells us, upon the authority of Walter Moyle,
" that the Society paid Dryden £40 for this sublime
" Ode, which, from the passage in his letter above
" quoted, seems to have been more than the bard ex-
" pected at commencing his labour. The music for
" this celebrated poem was originally composed by

" Jeremiah Clarke, one of the Stewards of the festival,
" whose productions were more remarkable for deep
" pathos and delicacy, than for fire and energy. It is
" probable that, with such a turn of mind and taste, he
" may have failed in setting the sublime, lofty, and
" daring flights of the Ode to St. Cecilia."* Sir
Walter goes on to observe, that Clarke's " composition
" was not judged worthy of publication." But no conclusion unfavourable to the composer can be fairly
drawn from the fact of his work not being published,
inasmuch as none of the odes produced between 1684
and 1703 were printed, although portions of them occasionally found their way into the publications of the
period. It may, however, be inferred, from the circumstance of no manuscript copy of Clarke's composition
being known to exist, that his efforts were attended
with only partial success. But however this may have
been, the composer and his professional colleague, Le
Riche, shortly afterwards announced the ode for public
performance in these terms :—" The Song composed
" by Mr. Jeremiah Clarke and sung on St. Cecilia's
" day will be performed on Thursday next at Mr. Hick-
" ford's Dancing School in Panton Street, or in James
" Street over against the Tennis-court, just by the Blue
" Posts, there being a door out of each street to the
" room ;† and for the benefit of the said Mr. Clarke

---

* *Life of Dryden*, edit. 1834, p. 345.

† This is perhaps the earliest notice to be found of this
room, which continued to be used for concerts, balls, and other
public entertainments for nearly a century. About 1730,
Hickford, or more likely his son, opened a room in Brewer

" and Mr. Le Riche, late Stewards of the said Feast.
" The musick begins at 8." (*London Gazette*, No.
3346, Monday, December 6, 1697.) And in the following week a second performance was advertised as
follows :—" The Song which was sung on St. Cecilia's
" day will be performed in York Buildings on Thurs-
" day next, the 16th inst. with an addition of a new
" Pastoral on the Peace,* composed by Mr. Jere-
" miah Clarke, and for the benefit of Mr. Le Riche
" only. The musick begins at 8." (*London Gazette*,
No. 3348, Monday, December 13, 1697.) The poem
was published separately, in folio, in December, 1697,
and whatever doubts may exist as to the success of the
music, it is certain that " the poetry received, even in
" the author's time, all the applause which its unrivalled
" excellence demanded. ' I am glad to hear from all
" hands,' says Dryden, in a letter to Tonson, ' that my

Street, Golden Square, as a dancing academy, which was frequently used for concerts.   This latter room still exists, and
is, or was recently, occupied as a dancing school.

    * The peace alluded to (that of Ryswick) appears to have
stimulated the composers of the day to active exertion.
Amongst the occasional pieces produced may be instanced, an
anthem, " Praise the Lord, O my soul," composed by Dr.
Blow, and performed on the Thanksgiving day, December
2nd, when the choir of St. Paul's was first opened for Divine
service (for which ceremonial Blow also wrote an anthem,
with instrumental accompaniments, " I was glad ") ;—an occasional interlude called " Europe's Revels on the Peace," written
by Peter Motteux, and set by John Eccles, performed at Lincoln's Inn Fields Theatre; and an Entertainment of music
composed by Vaughan Richardson, organist of Winchester Cathedral, and performed in February, 1697-8, at York Buildings.

" Ode is esteemed the best of all my poetry, by all the
" town. I thought so myself when I writ it; but,
" being old, I mistrusted my own judgment.' Mr.
" Malone has preserved a tradition that the father of
" Lord Chief Justice Marlay, then a Templar, and
" frequenter of Will's Coffee House, took an opportunity
" to pay his court to Dryden, on the publication of
" Alexander's Feast; and happening to sit next him,
" congratulated him on having produced the finest and
" noblest Ode that had ever been written in any lan-
" guage. ' You are right, young gentleman (replied
" Dryden), a nobler Ode never *was* produced, nor ever
" *will*.' This singularly strong expression cannot be
" placed to the score of vanity. It was an inward con-
" sciousness of merit, which burst forth probably almost
" involuntarily, and I fear must be admitted as pro-
" phetic." (Scott's *Life of Dryden*, 348.) Sir John
Hawkins (*History of Music*, iv. 522,) mentions a report,
" that Dryden wrote his Alexander's Feast with a view
" to its being set by Purcell, but that Purcell declined
" the task, as thinking it beyond the power of music to
" express sentiments so superlatively energetic as that
" ode abounds with." He however questions the cor-
rectness of the statement, because, he says, " Purcell
" composed the Te Deum, and scrupled not to set to
" music some of the most sublime passages in the
" Psalms, the Prophecy of Isaiah, and other parts of
" Holy Scripture," &c. But it is strange that it should
have altogether escaped the memory of the worthy
knight, that at the time Alexander's Feast was written,
Purcell had been dead for nearly two years.

A. D. 1698.—The first incident met with this year in connection with the subject of our inquiries is the announcement of one of Dr. Blow's odes as the prominent feature of a benefit concert; the usual medium of communication, the Gazette, informing us as follows:—" On Tuesday next, the 10th instant, will be performed " in York-buildings an entertainment of vocal and in- " strumental musick, being St. Cecilia's Song, com- " posed by Dr. Blow, and several other new songs for " the benefit of Mr. Bowman and Mr. Snow." (No. 3390, May 9th, 1698.) A still further increase of rent was this year demanded by the officers of the Stationers' Company, on the ground of the damage done to the Hall; a compromise was however effected, as appears by the entry in one of the Company's books (G. 16, a.) of an order that " the Hall should be let to " the Stewards of St. Cecilia's feast for five pounds, " they agreeing to make good all damage that may " happen to it or any room adjoining." The meeting was twice advertised in the *London Gazette* (Nos. 3443 and 3444, November 10th and 14th, 1698), in the following terms:—" The Anniversary Feast of the " Society of Gentlemen, Lovers of Musick, will be kept " at Stationers-Hall on St. Cecilia's day being Tuesday " the 22nd instant. Tickets to be delivered at Mr. " Ric. Glover's at the Castle Tavern in Fleet Street, " Mr. Benj. Tooke's at the Middle Temple Gate, the " Rose Tavern in Covent Garden,* and Garaway's

---

* Benjamin Tooke was a bookseller and publisher. The Rose Tavern was in Bridges Street; its site is now occupied by part of Drury Lane Theatre.

" Coffee House near the Royal Exchange." The ode for this year's celebration was written by Thomas Bishop,* and composed by Daniel Purcell. The music cannot be found, but the poem (an exceedingly poor performance) is still extant. It has been seen that the professors of music who acted as Stewards at the last festival, had the ode performed at a concert for their benefit shortly after its production. The following advertisement would appear to warrant the belief that their example was followed by those who officiated in the same capacity in the present year. " On Wednes-
" day next will be performed in York-buildings Mr.
" Daniel Purcell's musick made for last St. Cecilia's
" feast, for the benefit of Mr. Howell and Mr. Shore,
" with an addition of new vocal and instrumental mu-
" sick, beginning at 7 at night." (*London Gazette*, No. 3458, January 2nd, 1698-9.)

A. D. 1699.—The advertisement announcing this year's meeting informs us that the tickets were to be delivered " at Mr. Richard Glover's at the Castle " Tavern in Fleet Street, at Ozinda's Chocolate House " near St. James's Gate, and at Garraway's Coffee " in Exchange Alley in Cornhill. The church service was on this occasion performed at St. Paul's ; the sermon being preached by Dr. William Sherlock (then Dean of the Cathedral, Master of the Temple, and

---

* All that is known of this writer is that he was of Wadham College, Oxford, and graduated as Master of Arts on the 26th of June, 1683.

chaplain to the king,) the father of Thomas Sherlock, afterwards Bishop of London. His text was Psalm lxxxi, verses 1 and 2. This discourse was shortly afterwards " Published at the Request of the Stewards." The ode, written by Theophilus Parsons, the author of the ode for 1693, has been preserved, but neither the music nor the name of the composer is known. The *London Gazette*, No. 3556, Monday, December 11th, contains the following announcement :—" On Wednes-" day next, the 13th instant, will be performed at York-" buildings, a Consort of Musick, with the last St. " Cecilia's Song ; for the benefit of Mr. Pate and Mr. " Purcell ; beginning exactly at 8 at night." The " last " St. Cecilia's Song," probably referred to that performed in London, although it may have meant the ode produced this year at Oxford, which was composed by Daniel Purcell, one of the concert-givers.

A. D. 1700.—The various means hitherto resorted to by the Society to avert the payment of a larger rent for the use of Stationers' Hall proved this year unavailing ; the sum of six guineas being now demanded and paid. The following advertisement of the festival appeared in the *London Gazette* of November 18th (No. 3654). " The Anniversary Meeting of the Society of Gentle-" men, Lovers of Musick, will be kept at Stationers' " Hall on St. Cecilia's day, being Friday the 22nd " instant. Tickets to be delivered at Mr. Ric. Glover's " at the Castle Tavern in Fleet Street ; Mr. Benj. " Tooke's at the Middle Temple Gate ; the Rose Tavern " in Covent Garden ; White's Chocolate House near

" St. James's; the Bell Tavern in King Street in
" Westminster;* the College Coffee House near the
" Church Yard, Westminster; and Garraway's Coffee
" House near the Royal Exchange." This was the
last time the advertisements of the meeting appeared in
the *Gazette.* To that publication they had theretofore
been confined, but this year they were also inserted in
the newspapers, the above announcement appearing in
the *Postman* of November 16-19. D'Urfey and Blow
were again associated in the production of the ode for
this year, concerning which an advertisement in the
Post-Boy (November 19-21,) says: " There is now
" published the Ode for St. Cecilia, set to musick by
" Dr. John Blow, the words made by Mr. D'Urfey.
" Printed for H. Playford. Price 2*d.*" This, of course,
means the words only. No copy of this publication has
been met with, nor was the ode reprinted in the author's
works. There are still extant, however, two undated
odes of Dr. Blow's composition, one of which was doubtless written for this year's festival.† The *Postman* of
November 23rd records the celebration in the following
paragraph: " Yesterday St. Cecilia's feast was kept at
" Stationers' Hall, where there was a very fine enter-
" tainment of musick, both there and at St. Bride's
" Church." Daniel Williams, the bass singer, soon

---

* Mention is made of this tavern in 1465, and it probably
existed at a much earlier period.

† MS. scores of these compositions are now in the library
of Dr. Rimbault; one of them is contained in a volume of
manuscript music formerly belonging to Dr. Croft, and dated,
in his handwriting, 1700.

E

afterwards issued this announcement: " A Consort of
" Vocal and Instrumental Musick, Composed by Dr.
" John Blow for the late Anniversary Feast of St. Ce-
" cilia, will be performed at Mr. Reason's Musick
" Room in York Buildings, on Wednesday the 11th
" instant at 8 in the evening, for the benefit of Mr. Dan.
" Williams. Tickets may be had at Wells's Coffee
" House at Scotland Yard Gate, and the Rainbow Coffee
" House at the Temple Gate." (*London Gazette*, No.
3659, December 5th, 1700.)

A. D. 1701.—Congreve wrote the ode for 1701,
which was set to music by John Eccles, Master of the
Queen's Band of Music, and the most popular dramatic
composer then living.* His composition has not descended to us in a complete form, but an idea of its
merits may be obtained from the detached portions of
it printed in the collection of the author's songs. These
pieces are five in number, consisting of a duet, " Wise
Nature owns;" a song for a bass voice, " Thy voice,
O Harmony;" and three other songs, the voice parts
of which are printed in the G clef, but one of which is
apparently designed for a tenor voice, viz., " Thou only,

---

* The names of Congreve and Eccles so frequently appear in
conjunction as poet and composer, as to lead to the supposition
of a close intimacy having subsisted between them. Besides the
above-mentioned ode, Eccles composed music for the songs in
Congreve's comedies of " Love for Love," and " The Way of
the World," and for his opera, " Semele." The latter piece,
however, was never performed. He was also, as before stated,
one of the successful competitors for the prizes given for the
composition of the " Judgment of Paris."

Goddess ;" " Ah ! sweet repose ;" and " See the for-
saken fair." The poem was published in 1702, by
Jacob Tonson, under the title of " A Hymn to Har-
" mony, Written in honour of St. Cecilia's Day, 1701.
" By Mr. Congreve. Set to Musick by Mr. John
" Eccles, Master of Her Majesties Musick."

A. D. 1702.—No certain information can be obtained
as to the performances at this year's meeting, but there
are circumstances which seem to warrant the conclusion
that an ode composed by William Norris, Master of the
choristers of Lincoln Cathedral, was then produced.*
The original manuscript of this ode was in the possession of Dr. Samuel Arnold, and afterwards of Benjamin
Jacob, the organist. It was disposed of, with the rest
of Mr. Jacob's library, by auction, in 1830. Its subsequent ownership has not been traced, although diligent inquiry has been made for it. A correspondent of
the *Harmonicon* in 1831, who had seen the manuscript,

---

* William Norris was one of the children of the Chapel-
royal at the time of the coronation of James II. in 1685. He
subsequently became Master of the choristers, and (according
to some authorities) Organist of Lincoln Cathedral. It is
doubtful, however, whether he ever held the latter appointment. In the collection of words of anthems published by
Dr. Croft in 1712, under the title of *Divine Harmony*, Norris
is described as " late Master of the Children, and one of
" the Cathedral Church at Lincoln." One of his anthems,
" Blessed are those," was printed in Playford's *Divine Com-
panion* and other collections, and other anthems and a service
composed by him are extant in manuscript. The date of his
death is not known, but it is supposed he must have been dead
at the time of Croft's publication.

described the composition as undated, and added, that as far as he remembered, the words indicated that it was written during a year of war. The year 1702 was of such a description. The exiled king, James II., died on 16th November, 1701, and the claims of his son to the English throne being recognized by Louis XIV., led to the dismissal of the French ambassador from London, and the recall of the English ambassador from Paris. Various other causes contributed to embroil other European states, and during this position of affairs William III. died on 8th March, 1702. On the 4th of May following, war was declared against France and Spain by England, the German Empire, and Holland. In June, Marlborough took the field as general of the allied armies, and despite of many obstacles, obliged the enemy to retreat in all quarters, and terminated a most successful campaign by the sieges and captures of Venloo, Ruremond, Stevenswaert, and Liege. The naval successes were equally important, and raised in a high degree the spirit of the people. The 12th November was appointed as a day of general thanksgiving, and Queen Anne and both Houses of Parliament went in state to St. Paul's, to return thanks " for the signal successes vouchsafed to Her Majesties " forces by sea and land, under the command of the " Earl of Marlborough in the Low Countries, and " James, Duke of Ormond, General, and Sir George " Rook, Admiral, at Vigo :—as also to those of her " Allies engaged in the present war against France and ." Spain, and likewise for the Recovery of the Prince of

" Denmark." * The present seems to have been (with one exception) the sole occasion of any allusion to passing political events finding its way into the Cecilian odes, which had theretofore been, and afterwards were confined entirely to the celebration of the praise of music. The exception referred to is a short ode written some time during the reign of Queen Anne, and set to music by George Holmes, Organist of Lincoln Cathedral ; † which contains an allusion to the then existing war. The words only of this ode have been found, but the name of the author is not given, nor is there any indication whatever as to the year or place of performance.

A. D. 1703.—John Hughes was the writer of this year's ode, the music for which was composed by Philip Hart, organist of St. Andrew Undershaft, and St. Michael's, Cornhill, and subsequently of St. Dionis Backchurch.‡ Hart's composition was published, shortly

---

* The sermon on this occasion was preached by Sir Jonathan Trelawney, Bishop of Exeter (formerly Bishop of Bristol, and afterwards Bishop of Winchester), one of the seven prelates who were committed to the Tower by James II. in 1688, and the subject of the celebrated Cornish ballad, " A good sword and a trusty hand."

† But little is known of this composer. Two anthems of his composition (one of them written on occasion of the Union of England and Scotland) are contained in the fifth volume of the Tudway collection. (Harleian MS. 7341.) The words of these and other anthems by him may be seen in Dr. Croft's *Divine Harmony*, 1712.

‡ Sir John Hawkins (*History of Music*, v. 178) conjectures

after its production, in quarto, under the title of " An
" Ode in Praise of Musick, set for variety of Voices
" and Instruments by Mr. Philip Hart; written by J.
" Hughes :" being the first ode that was printed entire
subsequently to that of Dr. Blow in 1684. A manuscript score of it, bearing the composer's signature, and
entitled " An Ode to Harmony," is now in the possession of Mr. Joseph Warren.

This was the last of the regular annual series of celebrations of St. Cecilia's day in London. Of the causes
of the discontinuance of a festival which had been held,
almost uninterruptedly, for twenty-one successive years,
no account can now be given. Whether the " Society
of Gentlemen, Lovers of Musick " gradually decayed,
or the expences of the festival increased so much, that
the receipts became inadequate to defray them, are matters which can only be conjectured. The war in which
the country was then engaged was doubtless not without its influence on the meetings, and before peace was
restored an event had taken place, which, by turning
the attention of the musical world to a new and more

---

him to have been the son of James Hart, gentleman of the
Chapel-royal, who is mentioned as one of the singers in the
ode for 1687. " He was," (says the historian) " a sound mu-
" sician, but entertained little relish for those refinements in
" music which followed the introduction of the Italian opera
" into this country, for which reason he was the idol of the
" citizens, especially such of them as were old enough to
" remember Blow and Purcell. He was a grave and decent
" man, remarkable for his affability and gentlemanly deport-
" ment." In another place Hawkins mentions his excessive
use of the shake in his organ playing. He died about 1750,
at a very advanced age.

attractive object, rendered a revival of the "Musick feasts" almost an impracticability. That event was the introduction into this country of the Italian opera. One portion of the celebration alone continued to be regularly kept up, viz., the sermon at St. Bride's. James Paterson in his *Pietas Londinensis*, published in 1714, speaking of St. Bride's Church, mentions as amongst the then existing institutions there, " A Musick-Sermon " on St. Cecilia's day, or November 23, given now by " private Gentlemen of the Parish, but formerly it was " kept up by the Company of Musicians and Parish " Clerks in London." By the " Company of Musicians " Paterson probably intended the Musical Society by which the festivals were conducted, unless we are to understand that on the discontinuance of the festival either the Company of Musicians, or that of Parish Clerks, or both jointly, had undertaken the charge of the annual sermon, and continued to provide for its delivery until some short time before the publication of his book.

But although the " Musick feast " no longer continued to be annually kept up by any associated body in the metropolis, its memory survived, and its usefulness was, no doubt, recognized amongst many of the professors of the tuneful art and others, and we consequently find, from time to time, odes written and composed in praise of music, and occasionally brought forward, sometimes on St. Cecilia's day, sometimes at other periods, by the more enthusiastic votaries of the lyre.

These occasional celebrations will now be brought under notice.

CHAPTER III.

London Celebrations continued.

A. D. 1708.

IN this year Pope (at the request of Mr., afterwards Sir Richard, Steele) wrote his well-known " Ode for Musick on St. Cecilia's day "—the finest production of that kind which has appeared since those of Dryden. In Spence's *Anecdotes* Pope is related to have thus expressed himself on the subject of this piece:—" Many " people would like my Ode on Musick better if Dry-" den had never written on that subject. It was at the " request of Mr. Steele that I wrote mine; and not " with any thought of rivalling that great man, whose " memory I do, and have always reverenced." Steele's reason for inducing Pope to undertake the writing of this ode is nowhere stated, but it may be surmised that inasmuch as two or three years afterwards he was known to be the proprietor of the concert-room in York Buildings, and was engaged in giving concerts there, he had at this time some interest in that building, and possibly contemplated a revival there of the custom of celebrating St. Cecilia's day. Pope's ode, however, does not appear to have been at this time set to music.

A. D. 1711.—The year 1711 was marked by an occurrence which though not a celebration of St. Cecilia's day, is too intimately connected with the subject to be passed over in an account of those festivals. Upon the arrival of Handel in England in the year 1710, and the highly successful representation of his opera of " Rinaldo " at the Opera-house in the Haymarket, the managers of Drury Lane Theatre deemed it prudent to desist from the production of operas at that house ; a determination which necessarily occasioned the dismissal of the persons who had hitherto been engaged in furnishing the theatre with such pieces. The discarded composers and adapters (Thomas Clayton, Nicola Francesco Haym, and Charles Dieupart *) thereupon endeavoured

---

* Thomas Clayton had been one of the royal band of music in the reign of William and Mary. Having travelled into Italy, and brought thence a collection of opera airs, he associated himself with Haym and Dieupart, both good musicians, in the task of adapting these airs to English words, and introducing them into operas. He also composed additional songs for these pieces, as well as the whole of the music for Addison's opera of " Rosamond." As a composer he is beneath notice.

Nicola Francesco Haym, a Roman by birth, was a performer on the violoncello, and a composer of some ability. He was also author of two Italian tragedies, a work on Ancient Medals, and of a History of Music. About the year 1730, he published proposals for printing, by subscription, an English translation of the latter work, but owing to want of encouragement, it never appeared.

Charles Dieupart, a Frenchman, was a fine performer on the violin and harpsichord. Upon the failure of the attempt of himself and colleagues to carry on concerts in York Buildings, he entered the opera band. He died about the year 1740.

to establish a concert at York Buildings, and in this speculation, Steele, then the proprietor of the concert-room, joined. To assist in carrying on the speculation, it was determined that Clayton should reset Dryden's " Alexander's Feast," and that matchless production being considered by the speculators as not well-adapted, in its original form, for music (notwithstanding its having been written expressly for that purpose), they conceived the bold idea of getting it altered. Steele accordingly wrote to Hughes, the poet, as follows:—
" Dear Sir, Mr. Clayton and I desire you, as soon
" as you can conveniently, to alter this Poem for
" Musick, preserving as many of Dryden's words
" and Verses as you can. It is to be perform'd by
" a Voice well-skill'd in Recitative, but you under-
" stand all these matters much better than Your af-
" fectionate humble Servant, R. Steele." Hughes complied with this request, and made numerous altera-tions in Dryden's noble poem. These alterations are stigmatized by Sir Walter Scott as " impertinent," and are thus strongly spoken of by Dr. Brown in his *Dis-sertation on Poetry and Music:*—" He [Hughes] had
" not sufficiently estimated his own strength when he
" attempted to tamper with the bow of Ulysses. When-
" ever he hath attempted a change he hath quenched
" the poetic fire." Clayton's composition was first per-formed at York Buildings, in conjunction with " The
" Passion of Sappho," a poem by Harrison, for which Clayton had also written music, on 24th May, 1711. It was twice repeated (the last time on 16th July), but
" did not satisfy the connoisseurs in musick." Hughes

(himself a musician*), writing to Steele after the first performance, thus expresses his opinion of the music:—
" The symphonies in many places seem to me perplexed,
" and not to pursue any subject or point. The over-
" ture of Alexander ought to be great and noble; in-
" stead of which I find only a hurry of the instruments,
" not proper, in my poor opinion, and without any
" design or fugue; and, I am afraid, perplexed and
" irregular in the composition, as far as I have any
" ideas or experience. Enquire this of better judgments.
" The duet of Bacchus is cheerful and has a good
" effect, but that beginning, ' Cupid, Phœbus, &c.' I
" cannot think shews any art, and is in effect no more
" than a single air. Nothing shews both genius and
" learning more than this sort of composition; the
" chief beauty of which consists in giving each voice
" different points, and making those points work toge-
" ther, and interchange regularly and surprisingly; or
" one point following itself in both the voices, in a kind
" of canon as it is called. These artfulnesses when
" well executed, give infinite delight to the ear, but
" that which I have mentioned is not formed after those
" designs; but where the voices join, they move ex-
" actly together in plain counterpoint, which shews
" little more than a single air. I think the words in
" general naturally enough expressed, and in some
" places pathetically; but because you seem to think
" this the whole mystery of setting, I take this oppor-

---

* Hawkins says he played the violin at the concerts of Thomas Britton, the famous musical small-coal man.

" tunity to assure you that it is as possible to express
" words naturally and pathetically in very faulty com-
" position as it is to hit a likeness in a bad picture.
" If the musick in score, without the words, does not
" prove itself by the rules of composition, which relate
" to the harmony and motion of different notes at the
" same time, the notes in the singing parts will not
" suffice though they express the words ever so natu-
" rally. This is properly the art of composition, in
" which there is room to shew admirable skill, abstracted
" from the words ; and in which the rules for the union
" of sounds are a kind of syntaxis, from which no one
" is allowed to err. I do not apply this last particular
" to any thing, but only to give you a general idea of
" what is composition. Yet, upon the whole, as far as
" I am able to judge, the musick of Sappho, and Alex-
" ander, though in some places agreeable, will not please
" masters." Clayton's music to Alexander's Feast has
long since passed into oblivion ; but some of his operas,
which are still extant, sufficiently attest the utter absence
of ability in this pretender to the rank of composer.
Although Stationers' Hall was no longer the scene of
the meetings of an important musical body on St. Cecilia's day, it was not altogether silent on that anniversary. This year a musical professor advertises in
the *Spectator* (No. 224, November 16th), as follows :—
" For the Benefit of Mr. Anthony Young, Organist of
" St. Clements Danes,* at Stationers' Hall on Thurs-

---

* This person was the composer of a collection of songs,
published in 1707. He had three daughters, all of whom be-

" day the 22nd instant, being St. Cœcilia's day, will be
" performed a Consort of Vocal and Instrumental Mu-
" sick, most of which will be entirely new ; and Mr.
" Leveridge sings that celebrated song, beginning ' Ge-
" nius of England.' Tickets are to be had at St. James's
" Coffee House, Tom's in Devereux Court, John's in
" Sweeting's Alley, and at Charles Lillie's at the Corner
" of Beaufort Buildings in the Strand at 5s. each."

A. D. 1717.—A musical entertainment of some kind
was composed for St. Cecilia's day this year by William
Babel.* No record, however, of any performance of it
on that day has been discovered. In the following year it
was announced for performance at Lincoln's Inn Fields
Theatre, thus :—" For the benefit of Mr. Babel. By
" the Company of Comedians. At the Theatre in Little
" Lincolns Inn Fields, this present Saturday, being the

---

came eminent as singers. Cecilia, the eldest, married Dr.
Arne, Isabella, the second, became the wife of John Frederick
Lampe, and Esther, the youngest, married Mr. Jones.

* This composer was the son of a musician who played the
bassoon at Drury Lane Theatre until he was eighty years of
age. He was taught music by his father, but studied composition under Dr. Pepusch. He became an excellent player
on the harpsichord, for which instrument he arranged numerous lessons from the Italian operas of the day ; amongst
others, a set from Handel's "Rinaldo." He was one of the Band
of music to George I., and in November, 1718, was appointed
organist of the united parishes of Allhallows and St. John the
Evangelist, Bread Street. He composed several concertos
and solos for instruments. He died at Canonbury House,
Islington, 23rd September, 1723, aged thirty-three, and was
buried in the church of which he was organist.

" 26th of April, will be presented a Play call'd 'The Jew
" of Venice.' In which will be perform'd an Entertain-
" ment of Vocal and Instrumental Musick for the late
" St. Cecilia's day, composed by Mr. Babel. With
" several Solos on the Harpsichord to be perform'd by
" him. The Vocal parts to be perform'd by Mrs. Bar-
" bier, Mr. Leveridge, and Mr. Babel's Scholar. With
" several Entertainments of Dancing by Mons. Moreau,
" Mr. Thurmond, Mrs. Bullock, and Miss Smith. Boxes
" 5s. Pit 3s. Gallery 2s. And on Monday next will
" be presented a Play call'd Don Sebastian, King of
" Portugal. To which will be added A New Farce
" call'd ' The Hypochondriack.' For the benefit of Mr.
" Hall and Mr. Griffin." The " Jew of Venice" mentioned in this advertisement was an alteration of Shakspere's play of " The Merchant of Venice," made by
George, Lord Lansdown. It was produced in 1701,
and kept possession of the stage until Macklin restored
the original play in 1741. In the second act a musical
masque, called " Peleus and Thetis" (the production of
Lord Lansdown), was introduced. It is probable that
on the occasion of Babel's benefit his entertainment
" for the late St. Cecilia's day" was temporarily sub-
stituted for the masque.

A. D. 1723.—On St. Cecilia's day, 1723, there was
produced at the theatre in Lincoln's Inn Fields a
musical entertainment, entitled " The Union of the
" Three Sister Arts," the music for which was composed by Dr. Pepusch. In this piece the sister arts of
Poetry, Painting, and Music are personified by Homer,

Apelles, and St. Cecilia, which characters were represented by Leveridge, La Guerre, and Mrs. Chambers.*
The piece was very successful, having been repeated on
Monday 25th and Saturday 30th November, and on
Friday 5th, Saturday 13th, and Thursday 18th December, when it gave place to the famous pantomime, " The
" Necromancer; or, Harlequin Dr. Faustus," which
was produced on Saturday, 20th December, and ran
for forty nearly consecutive nights. On one of the
nights on which the pantomime was laid aside (Friday,
2nd January), " The Union of the Three Sister Arts "
was again performed. This entertainment was never
printed, but the music (consisting of the overture, four
songs, two duets, and two chorusses) was published in
score in the December following its production.

A. D. 1725.—On St. Cecilia's day in this year, the
same entertainment was reproduced at Lincoln's Inn
Fields Theatre; being then announced as " a Masque of
" Musick call'd St. Cecilia, or The Union of the Three
" Sister Arts. St. Cecilia, Mrs. Chambers; Homer,
" Mr. Leveridge; Apollo [by mistake for Apelles],
" Mr. Legar. With proper dances to be perform'd by
" Mons. Salle, Mons. Dupre, Mr. Lally, Mrs. Wall,
" Mrs. Bullock and Mrs. Anderson." It was repeated
on Monday, 29th November.

---

* These three performers were constantly employed in the
musical pieces and pantomimes produced at Lincoln's Inn
Fields Theatre, and afterwards at Covent Garden Theatre for
many years after this time.

A. D. 1730.—In this year the ode which Pope had written for 1708, was first set to music, but neither for any celebration of St. Cecilia's day, nor in the form in which it was produced by its author. The circumstances under which this took place were these:—Maurice Greene, being about to take the degree of Doctor in Music at the University of Cambridge, chose this ode for composition as his exercise, and, probably finding it, in its original form, too long for his purpose, applied to Pope to alter and adapt it for him. Pope, complying with Greene's request, thereupon made extensive alterations in the poem. He reduced its length about one third, by the excision of the entire latter part, and introduced a new stanza, besides making considerable modifications in the first part. When thus changed, Greene composed music for the ode, which was performed at the Music Act, at the Public Commencement at Cambridge, on Monday, July 6th, 1730.* This music yet remains in manuscript, with the exception of one duet, printed in the fifth volume of Hawkins' *History of Music.* The altered poem was first printed at the end of a pamphlet published at Cambridge in this year, with the title of " Questiones, una " cum carminibus, in Magnis Comitiis Cantabrigiæ cele- " bratis, 1730."† In 1740 it was included in *A*

---

* Besides conferring on Greene the degree of Doctor in Music, the University, in the same year, on the death of Dr. Tudway, appointed him their Professor of Music.

† This fact was first pointed out by Mr. Bolton Corney in May, 1855, in a communication to *Notes and Queries,* vol. xi. p. 360.

Miscellany of Lyric Poems, the greatest part written for, and perform'd in the Academy of Music, held in the Apollo.* In 1776, it was given by Hawkins (who laboured under an erroneous impression that it had never before appeared in print) in his *History of Music,* but it has not yet been included in any edition of Pope's works. There is nothing to show at what period Greene's music was first performed in London beyond the *Miscellany of Lyric Poems* just mentioned, but it was probably brought forward soon after its production at Cambridge.

A. D. 1736.—In this year an important event in connexion with the Cecilian odes happened ; viz. the composition of new music for Dryden's "Alexander's Feast," by no less celebrated a composer than Handel. In the year 1733, Handel, then the musical director of the Opera House, having refused to submit to the caprices of Senesino, the singer, was violently opposed by a large party of the nobility and gentry, who, espousing the cause of the vocalist, opened a second opera house under Porpora at Lincoln's Inn Fields Theatre. At the end of a season Handel retreated from the Opera House in the Haymarket, which was immediately occupied by the opposition party under Porpora. Handel

---

* The Apollo was a large room in the Devil Tavern at Temple Bar, where concerts were held, and where Greene, after his secession from the Academy of Ancient Music in 1731, established a rival concert, which was, most likely, that to which the designation " Academy of Music " on the title of the *Miscellany of Lyric Poems* is applied.

F

thereupon commenced the performance of operas at the
newly erected theatre in Covent Garden, but found
himself at the termination of the season, not only bank-
rupt in fortune, but so severely affected in health as to
be necessitated to seek relief from the baths of Aix-la-
Chapelle. His departure and future intentions are thus
recorded in one of the newspapers in May, 1735 :—
" Mr. Handel goes to spend the summer in Germany,
" but comes back against Winter and is to have Con-
" certs of Musick next Season, but no Operas." In
the ensuing October the public were prepared for his
return by the following paragraph :—" We hear that
" Mr. Handell will perform Oratorios and have Con-
" certs of Musick this Winter at Covent Garden Thea-
" tre." On his return he applied himself to preparing
for the approaching season, and composed his music to
" Alexander's Feast," which he completed, according
to his memorandum on the manuscript score, on 17th
January, 1736. This he brought out at Covent Garden Theatre on Thursday 19th February following ; the
principal singers being Signora Strada, Miss Young,*
the celebrated John Beard (who continued throughout
the remainder of Handel's career his principal tenor,
and for whom most of the tenor parts in his oratorios
were written), and Mr. Erard. The pit and boxes were
laid together at half a guinea each person ; the admis-

---

* This was Cecilia, the eldest daughter of Anthony Young
before mentioned, and afterwards the wife of Dr. Arne. She
was a pupil of Geminiani, and first appeared about the year
1730.

sion to the first gallery was four shillings, and to the second, half a crown. The great success of the ode is thus chronicled in *The London Daily Post and General Advertiser* of the day after its production :—" Last " night his Royal Highness the Duke, and her Royal " Highness the Princess Amelia were at the Theatre " Royal in Covent Garden, to hear Mr. Dryden's Ode, " set to Musick by Mr. Handel. Never was upon the " like Occasion, so numerous and splendid an Audience " at any Theatre in London, there being at least 1300 " Persons present ; and it is judg'd that the Receipt of " the House could not amount to less than 450*l.* It " met with general Applause ; though attended with " the Inconvenience of having the Performers placed at " too great a distance from the Audience, which we hear " will be rectified the next Time of Performance." It was repeated on the four succeeding nights of performance, when it was withdrawn to allow of two performances of Acis and Galatea, and two of Esther, which terminated the Lent Season. After Easter, Handel, departing from his intention to the contrary, resumed the performance of operas. After giving two representations of Ariodante, he produced Atalanta (written on occasion of the marriage of Frederick, Prince of Wales, with the Princess of Saxe Gotha), which ran for eight successive nights, and closed the season. It may be interesting to notice here the charges made to Handel for the theatre, which appear by the following entry in the Account of the Treasurer of Lincoln's Inn Fields and Covent Garden Theatres.

" Mr. Handel's Music.

Dr.	Charge				Nights paid for		Cr.
1735-6					1735-6		
Thursday							
Feby. 19	Alexander's Feast	52	5	8	Received ⎱ For Rent & Actors	90 0	0
Wed. 25	Alexander's Feast	52	5	8	Feb. 27 ⎰ Servants pr. list . 14	11	4
Mar. 3d	Alexander's Feast	52	5	8	Mar. 3 Received in full . . 52	5	8
Friday 12	Alexander's Feast	19	5	8	„ 12 Received in full . . 19	5	8
Wed. 17	Alexander's Feast	19	5	8	„ 17 Received in full . . 19	5	8
Wed. 24	Acis & Galatea	19	5	8	„ 24 Received in full . . 19	5	8
Wed. 31	Acis & Galatea	19	5	8	„ 31 Received in full . . 19	5	8
Wed. Apl. 7	Esther . . .	19	5	8	Apl. 7 Received in full . . 19	5	8
Wed. 14	Esther . . .	19	5	8	„ 14 Received in full . . 19	5	8
Wed. May 5th	Ariodante .	52	5	8	May 5 Received in full . . 52	5	8
Fri. 7	Ariodante .	52	5	8	„ 7 Received in full . . 52	5	8
Wed. 12	Atalanta .	52	5	8	„ 12 Received in full . . 52	5	8
Sat. 15	Atalanta .	52	5	8	„ 15 Received in full . . 52	5	8
Wed. 19	Atalanta .	52	5	8	„ 19 Received in full . . 52	5	8
Sat. 22	Atalanta .	52	5	8	„ 22 Received in full · . 52	5	8
Wed. 26	Atalanta .	52	5	8	„ 26 Received in full . . 52	5	8
Sat. 29	Atalanta .	52	5	8	„ 29 Received in full . . 52	5	8
Wed. June 2	Atalante .	52	5	8	June 2 Received in full . . 52	5	8
Wed. June 9	Atalante .	33	13	8	„ 19 Recd. 33	13	8."
	In all 19.						

The charges in this account may be thus explained :—
The rent of the theatre per night amount-

ed to	12	0	0
The charge for Servants, *i. e.* Door-			
keepers, &c.	7	5	8
Making together .	19	5	8

To which was added the amount of the
nightly salaries which the actors were entitled to receive from the manager for every
night on which the theatre was open during
the season, and on which dramatic per-

formances could have been given . .	33	0	0
Making a total of .	52	5	8

The reduction of the charge to £19 5s. 8d. for each of the six nights commencing 12th March and ending 14th April is owing to those nights being the Wednesdays and Fridays in Lent, when (as the theatre could not be opened for dramatic performances) the actors were not entitled to be paid their salaries. The reduction of the charge of £33 to £14 8s. on the 9th June cannot be accounted for.

It would appear from the original printed score of Handel's music to Alexander's Feast, that two additional chorusses, which were appended to the ode by Newburgh Hamilton (who was engaged by Handel to make the necessary division of the poem into recitatives, airs, and chorusses), and for which Handel composed music at the same time as for the original work, were not introduced at the first performances, but that Dryden's text was adhered to, the ode terminating with the chorus, "Let old Timotheus."* On the revival of the piece in the following season (March, 1737), not only were the additional chorusses performed, but an Italian cantata in praise of St. Cecilia, sung by Signora Strada and Signor Aragoni, a tenor; and an Italian song for Signor Annibali, a contralto, who came to England in the preceding October, were likewise appended. A new edition of the score, including all these additions, was " published by the Author" shortly

---

* This chorus is a remarkable instance of the manner in which Handel was accustomed to alter and adapt his earlier compositions. Three of its four subjects are taken from the Italian trio, " Quel fior che al alba ride;" the fourth alone (that first given out by the alto voice) being new.

afterwards. To the book of the words Hamilton attached the following Lines to Handel and preface.

" TO MR. HANDEL, ON HIS SETTING TO MUSICK
  MR. DRYDEN'S ' FEAST OF ALEXANDER.'

" Let others charm the list'ning scaly brood,
  Or tame the savage monsters of the wood ;
  With magick Notes inchant the leafy grove,
  Or force ev'n things inanimate to move :
  Be ever your's (my friend,) the God-like art
  To calm the passions, and improve the heart ;
  The tyrant's rage and hell-born pride controul,
  Or sweetly sooth to peace the mourning soul ;
  With martial warmth the hero's breast inspire,
  Or fan new-kindling love to chaste desire.
  That artist's hand (whose skill alone could move
  To glory, grief, or joy the son of Jove,)
  Not greater raptures to the Grecian gave,
  Than British theatres from you receive ;
  That ignorance and envy vanquish'd see ;
  Heav'n made, you rule the world by Harmony.
  Two glowing sparks of that celestial flame
  Which warms by mystick art this earthly frame,
  United in one blaze of genial heat,
  Produc'd this piece in sense and sounds complete ;
  The Sister Arts, as breathing from one soul,
  With equal spirit animate the whole.
  Had Dryden liv'd the welcome day to bless,
  Which cloth'd his numbers in so fit a dress ;
  When his majestick poetry was crown'd
  With all your bright magnificence of sound ;
  How would his wonder and his transport rise ?
  Whilst fam'd Timotheus yields to you the prize."

" PREFACE.

" The following Ode being universally allow'd to be
" the most excellent of its kind (at least in our lan-
" guage), all admirers of polite amusements have with

" impatience expected its appearing in a musical dress
" equal to the subject. But the late improvements in
" musick varying so much from that turn of composi-
" tion, for which this poem was originally design'd,
" most people despair'd of ever seeing that affair pro-
" perly accomplish'd : the alteration in the words (ne-
" cessary to render them fit to receive modern compo-
" sition) being thought scarcely practicable, without
" breaking in upon that flow of spirit which runs thro'
" the whole of the poem, which of consequence wou'd
" be render'd flat and insipid. I was long of this opi-
" nion, not only from a diffidence of my own capacity,
" but the ill success of some ingenious gentlemen,
" whose alterations of or additions to the original,
" prov'd equally ill-judg'd. But upon a more parti-
" cular review of the Ode, these seeming difficulties
" vanish'd ; tho' I was determin'd not to take any un-
" warrantable liberty with that poem, which has so long
" done honour to the nation ; and which no man can
" add to, or abridge, in any thing material, without
" injuring it : I therefore confin'd myself to a plain
" division of it into Airs, Recitative, or Chorus's ;
" looking upon the words in general so sacred, as
" scarcely to violate one in the order of its first place :
" How I have succeeded, the world is to judge ; and
" whether I have preserv'd that beautiful description of
" the passions, so exquisitely drawn, at the same time
" I strove to reduce them to the present taste in sounds.
" I confess my principal view was, not to lose this
" favourable opportunity of its being set to music by
" that great Master, who has with pleasure undertaken

" the task, and who only is capable of doing it justice;
" whose compositions have long shewn, that they can
" conquer even the most obstinate partiality, and in-
" spire life into the most senseless words. If this
" entertainment can, in the least degree, give satisfac-
" tion to the real judges of poetry or music, I shall
" think myself happy in having promoted it; being
" persuaded, that it is next to an improbability, to offer
" the world any thing in those arts more perfect than
" the united labours and utmost efforts of a Dryden and
" a Handel. N. H."

It may be mentioned here that in 1739, on the occasion of the first benefit concert for the Fund for the
relief of decayed Musicians (now called the Royal Society of Musicians), Handel's music to Alexander's
Feast was performed, with several concertos for the
organ and other instruments, and Dr. Arne's Judgment of Paris ; Handel giving the house and his own
performance gratis.

A. D. 1739.—In the autumn of 1739, Handel, having set to music Dryden's first Ode for St. Cecilia's
day—that originally set by Draghi in 1687—announced
(in the following advertisement) his intention of producing it on the anniversary of the Saint's festival.
" At the Theatre Royal in Lincoln's Inn Fields, on
" Thursday, the 22d of November (being St. Cecilia's
" day), will be perform'd A New Ode. With two new
" Concertos for several Instruments ; Which will be
" preceded by Alexander's Feast, and a Concerto on
" the Organ. Boxes, Half a Guinea; Pit, 5s.; First

" Gallery, 3s.; Upper Gallery, 2s. To begin at Six
" o'clock." And a few days before the performance it
is thus more particularly announced. " Lincoln's Inn
" Fields. At the Theatre Royal in Lincoln's Inn
" Fields, Thursday next, Nov. 22, (being St. Cecilia's
" Day), will be perform'd An Ode of Mr. Dryden's,
" with two new Concertos for several instruments.
" Which will be preceded by Alexander's Feast and a
" Concerto on the Organ. Boxes, Half a Guinea;
" Pit, 5s.; First Gallery, 3s.; Upper Gallery, 2s.
" *** Particular care is taken to have the house well
" air'd ; * and the Passage from the Fields to the House
" will be covered for better conveniency. To begin at
" Six o'Clock." The principal singers in the ode were
Signora Francesina and Mr. Beard. The performance
was repeated on Tuesday, 27th November, and on
Thursday, 13th December, the Ode was again performed in conjunction with " Acis and Galatea," and
" two new Concertos for several Instruments, never
" perform'd before." The advertisement of the latter
performance announces " Pit and Gallery Doors will be
" open'd at Four, the Boxes at Five. Particular Care
" will be taken to have Guards placed to keep all the
" Passages clear from the Mob." The same performance was repeated on 20th December, and again on
Thursday, 13th February, 1740. The Ode was again
performed in the following season, on the closing night

---

* The winter of 1739-40 was a remarkably severe one; the
Thames was frozen over from Christmas until near the end of
January, and a fair held, and an ox roasted whole upon it.

of which (8th April, 1741) it was given in combination with L'Allegro, Il Pensieroso ed Il Moderato, when the following curious notice was appended to the announcement in the *London Daily Post*. " N.B. This being " the last time of performing, many persons of quality " and others are pleased to make great demands for " Box Tickets, which encourages me, (and hope will " give no offence) to put the Pit and Boxes together, " at half a guinea each." This Ode is one of the numerous evidences of Handel's wonderful rapidity of composition. From his memoranda on the original score it appears that it occupied him but the short space of ten days, being commenced on the 15th, and finished on 24th September. Sir John Hawkins, in his *History of Music*, has stated (and his statement has been copied by later writers), that a great part of the music of this ode was originally composed for an opera entitled Alceste, written by Dr. Smollett, and set by Handel in fulfilment of an engagement with Rich, the manager of Covent Garden Theatre, and for which opera Rich incurred great expense in getting a set of scenes painted by the celebrated Servandoni ; but which was never performed. Mr. Mudie, in his preface to the edition of the ode, published by the Handel Society, observes with reference to this statement, that " the descriptive " character of the music, particularly of the intro- " ductory recitative and first chorus, and also of the " songs which follow until the last chorus, seems to be " a very strong evidence of its having been composed " to illustrate the poetry of Dryden." There is not, however, the slightest ground for any doubt upon the subject. The opera which Handel composed for Rich, and for which Servandoni painted the scenes— Alcides, not Alceste—is contained in the collection of Handel's Works edited by Dr. Arnold; the copy from which it was printed having been presented to Dr. Arnold by Colman the elder, who had succeeded Beard, the son-in-law of Rich, in the management of Covent Garden Theatre. A comparison of the scores of Alcides and the Ode for St. Cecilia's day will at once show that none of the music of the opera was adopted into the ode. The piece to which much of the music of Alcides was transferred was the Choice of Hercules, written in 1751.

A. D. 1740.—From the *Miscellany of Lyric Poems* published in this year (and already noticed under the date of 1730), it appears that amongst the pieces performed at this time at " the Academy of Music held in the Apollo," were three odes for St. Cecilia's day; viz., one, originally written by Addison, about 1692, for performance at Oxford, which was now re-set by Michael Christian Festing;* another, written by the Rev. Mr.

---

* Festing was a violinist of some note, who first appeared about 1724. He was a member of the king's band, and leader at many concerts. Upon the opening of Ranelagh, about 1743, he became director of the music there. He died in 1752. "As a performer on the violin (says Hawkins) Festing "was inferior to many of his time; but as a composer, parti-"cularly of solos for that instrument, the nature and genius "whereof he perfectly understood, he had but few equals." Festing likewise merits honourable remembrance as one of the founders of the Royal Society of Musicians.

Vidal, Under Master of Westminster School, and set to music by Mr. (afterwards Dr.) William Boyce; and the third written by John Lockman,* also set by Boyce. It cannot be discovered whether either of these compositions was performed on St. Cecilia's day. One of Boyce's compositions (the ode written by Lockman) obtained a more extended reputation than appears to have fallen to the lot of the others, since we find it announced for performance by the Philharmonic Society of Dublin, "at their Musick Room in Fishamble Street,"† in October, 1744. It has never been printed, but is believed to be still extant in manuscript. About the same time the unfortunate Christopher Smart produced an Ode for St. Cecilia's day, which, however, was not set to music until long after. It may also be mentioned that Smart translated Pope's ode into Latin verse, but without regard to conformity of measure.‡

---

* Lockman was Secretary to the British Herring Fishery. He was author of a few odes, songs, and other poems, chiefly intended for music, and of a musical drama, called " Rosa▪ linda," set to music by John Christopher Smith, and performed at Hickford's Great Room in Brewer Street. (Prefixed to the printed copy of this drama is, An Enquiry into the rise and progress of Operas and Oratorios, with some reflections on Lyric Poetry and music.) Lockman also wrote an oratorio, entitled, "David's Lamentation over Saul and Jonathan" (included in the before mentioned *Miscellany of Lyric Poems*), which was set to music by both Boyce and John Christopher Smith. He died 2nd February, 1771.

† In this room, which was opened in October, 1741, the first performance of Handel's " Messiah " took place on 13th April, 1742. The room was some years afterwards converted into a theatre.

‡ Smart was the son of the steward of Lord Vane, and was

A. D. 1749.—In this year Bonnell Thornton * (of whom it was said that, " like Dr. Arbuthnot, he amused " himself with laughing at the follies of the times with " a degree of pleasantry that entertained the public " without offending the individual at whom the ridicule " was aimed ") published a humorous burlesque upon the Cecilian odes, under the title of " An Ode on Saint " Cecilia's day, adapted to the Ancient British Mu- " sick :"—*i. e.* the salt-box, Jew's-harp, hurdy-gurdy, marrow-bones and cleavers, &c. This lively sally is said by Edward Jones (*Musical Relics of the Welch Bards*) to have been set to music with characteristic accompaniments by Dr. Arne, and performed on 22nd November, 1749, but this seems somewhat doubtful. The ode was, however, set to music in 1759 by Dr. Burney, and it was possibly to this composition that Jones intended to refer. Dr. Burney has given the following account of his work and its performance. " In " 1759 " (says he), " I set for Smart and Newbery, " Thornton's Burlesque Ode on St. Cecilia's day. It " was performed at Ranelagh in masks, to a very

---

born at Shipborne in Kent. He received his education at Pembroke College, Cambridge, where he took the degree of M.A. and obtained a fellowship, which however he vacated by marriage. Possessed of great abilities, both natural and acquired, he indulged in intemperate habits to such excess as to affect his reason. He died in 1771, having long suffered " the accumulated miseries of debt, disease, and insanity."

* This gentleman was born in Westminster about 1725, and educated in the school there, whence he removed to Christ Church, Oxford, where he took the degrees of M.A. in 1750, and B.M. in 1754. He died in 1768.

" crowded audience, as I was told, for I then resided in
" Norfolk.   Beard sang the Salt-box song, which was
" admirably accompanied on that instrument by Brent,
" the fencing master, and father of Miss Brent, the
" celebrated singer ; Skeggs on the broomstick as bas-
" soon, and a remarkable performer on the Jew's harp
" —' Buzzing twangs the iron lyre.'   Cleavers were
" cast in bell metal for this entertainment.   All the
" performers of the Old Woman's Oratory, employed
" by Foote, were, I believe, employed at Ranelagh on
" this occasion."   (See Boswell's *Life of Johnson*, edit.
1835, II. 197, Note.)   To the copy of this ode published by the author, the following amusing burlesque
preface was attached :—" My very singular modesty
" would never have permitted me to make the following
" Ode publick, had I not at length been overcome by
" the repeated solicitations of the Society wherein it
" was performed.   It may perhaps be expected that I
" should give some account of the musical instruments
" herein mentioned.   The Judaic, or (as it is commonly
" called) Jews Harp, speaks its origin in its appella-
" tion : and I cannot help thinking that this was the
" harp which David used, as the sound of the Hebrew
" language seems particularly adapted to this instru-
" ment.   I would therefore advise all painters, en-
" gravers, &c., not to represent the royal Psalmist with
" that many-stringed Welch harp in his hand, as they
" have hitherto done, but to place a monochord lyre in
" his mouth, such as was used by the Jews in his time,
" and by them transmitted down to us.   I am sorry I
" can give no certain account of those two incomparable

" instruments, the Salt-box, and the Hum-strum, or
" Bladder and String; tho' tis reasonable to conclude,
" that the first was usually performed on at Festivals,
" and the other on more serious occasions. The Mar-
" row-bones and Cleavers is undoubtedly our own inven-
" tion, and does honour to the British Nation. This
" was originally made use of in our wars; when our
" brave ancestors rush'd on their enemies (like the an-
" cient Gauls,) clashing their weapons, and ready to
" knock or cleave them down with those very instru-
" ments on which they could beat so terrible an alarm.
" Indeed since the pernicious introduction of fire-arms,
" the Marrow-bones and Cleavers have quitted the
" scenes of human slaughter, and now are confined to
" the shambles. But considering the degeneracy of
" the present age, we might not perhaps, from the
" small quantity of old English beef now consumed, be
" able to arm a sufficient number with that musical and
" warlike weapon, a Marrow-bone. If this Ode con-
" tributes in the least to lessen our false taste in admir-
" ing that foreign Musick now so much in vogue, and
" to recall the ancient British spirit, together with the
" ancient British harmony, I shall not think the pains
" I employed on the composition entirely flung away
" on my countrymen. This Ode, I am sensible, is not
" without faults; tho' I cannot help thinking it far
" superior to the Odes of Johnny Dryden, Jemmy Ad-
" dison, Sawney Pope, Nick Rowe, little Kit Smart,
" &c. &c. &c., or of any that have written or shall
" write on Saint Cecilia's day. FUSTIAN SACKBUT.
" I have strictly adher'd to the rule of making the

" sound echo to the sense." Jones has printed (in his *Musical Relics of the Welch Bards*) this ode from a copy published in 1763. In the preface (which is considerably altered and abridged from that given above) allusion is made to an intended performance at Ranelagh on 10th June in that year.

A. D. 1794.—In this year Samuel Wesley, the celebrated performer on the organ, composed music for an ode written upwards of a century before, by his grandfather, the Rev. Samuel Wesley, but it is believed that his composition was never performed. The original manuscript bearing the signature and memorandum, " S. Wesley, finished October 21, 1794, S. D. G." is now in the library of the British Museum (Add. MS. 14,339), to which institution it was presented in July, 1843, by Mr. Vincent Novello.

A. D. 1800.—About this period Christopher Smart's Ode was set to music by William Russell, Mus. Bac. Oxon.* Inquiry has failed to discover either the pre-

---

* William Russell, the son of an organ-builder, was born in London in the year 1777. Exhibiting early a talent for music, he commenced, at eight years of age, studying (chiefly the organ) under various masters, and at twelve years old was able to undertake the duties of a parochial organist. After being successively organist of a chapel in Great Queen Street, and of the church of St. Anne, Limehouse, he was appointed in 1801, organist to the Foundling Hospital. When about twenty years of age he placed himself under the tuition of Dr. Arnold, and in 1800 he was engaged, at Arnold's recommendation, as pianist and composer at Sadler's Wells. He

cise date of the composition, or the occasion of its production, but it is conjectured that it was written for,
and possibly performed on St. Cecilia's day by the
Cecilian Society, of which the composer was a member.
It seems pretty certain that it was performed by that
body at Painters' Hall, Little Trinity Lane, in the
latter part of the year 1800. This " Cecilian Society "
(which is still existing) was established in the year
1785, not, as might be supposed from its name, for the
purpose of reviving the celebrations on St. Cecilia's
day, but for the practice and performance of choral
music, to which attention had been greatly drawn by the
Commemoration of Handel held in the year preceding.
The members of this body have, however, been accustomed to hold a concert on St. Cecilia's day, and occasionally to call to recollection the former anniversary
celebrations by a performance of Handel's music to
Dryden's ode, " From harmony, from heav'nly harmony."

A musical society similarly named was in existence
about forty years before the establishment of the present
Cecilian Society, but no memorial of its proceedings has
been discovered beyond the following announcement,
which frequently appeared in the *Public Advertiser*

---

subsequently filled a similar situation at the Circus (now the
Surrey Theatre,) and Covent Garden Theatre. Russell composed two oratorios, " The Redemption of Israel," and " Job,"
and several odes, glees, songs, &c. His dramatic compositions,
about twenty in number, were chiefly spectacles and pantomimes. He died in the year 1813, at the age of 36, a period
of life which has proved fatal to many musicians; witness,
amongst others, Purcell, Pergolesi, Mozart, and Mendelssohn.

during the month of June, 1759:—" St. Cæcilian
" Society. The Subscribers are desired to take Notice
" that the Annual Meeting in the Long Room at
" Hampstead will be on Saturday, the 30th Instant.
" The Concert to begin at Eleven o'clock, and Dinner
" upon Table at Three. Subscribers Tickets are left
" with Mr. Rowden at the King's Arms in Cornhill."

This terminates the history of the Cecilian celebrations
in the metropolis, and we now proceed to notice the
establishment of festivals of a like nature in several of
the provincial towns of England and in the capitals of
Scotland and Ireland.

CHAPTER IV.

Provincial Celebrations.

Oxford.

ABOUT the same time as the musical celebrations on St. Cecilia's day were established in London, similar festivals were
instituted at Oxford. For many years
prior to this time the members of the University had
been distinguished for the assiduity with which they
cultivated the study and practice of music. Anthony à
Wood (in his *Life*) has left us a very particular account
of the weekly meetings for that purpose held by them
during the Protectorate and in the early part of the
reign of Charles II., and Sir John Hawkins (*History
of Music*, iv. 374) has printed some documents showing
how zealously they laboured to support their musical
establishments at a somewhat later period. With such
dispositions there can be no doubt that the idea of such
an annual gathering as the Cecilian celebrations, was
eagerly entertained and promptly carried into execution.

It is much to be regretted that but few particulars of
the Oxford celebrations can now be obtained. From
such as the writer has been able to collect, it appears

that the meetings resembled those held in London in the important features of attendance at a sermon and the performance of an ode. Stewards for conducting the festival were also appointed, as in the metropolis, and the meeting appears to have been carried on under the auspices of some associated body.

Scarcely any information of the persons engaged in the performances is now to be found. It may, however, be conjectured that the choirs of the various college chapels supplied the vocal performers, and that the band was composed of such professors as were resident in the city, together with the most efficient amateurs, and possibly a few players from London.

The first ode met with, which may be supposed to have been performed at Oxford, is one written in 1686, by a youth named Thomas Fletcher,* who had been a scholar at Winchester school, but had then recently become a student at New College. This ode is printed in a collection of the author's *Poems on several occasions*, published by him in 1692, and this is, unfortunately, all that can be ascertained respecting it, no

---

* Fletcher was probably a native of Fairfield, Somersetshire, of the donative of which (according to Wood) he was possessed, and whence he dates the dedication of his volume of *Poems on several occasions*. Judging from an expression in the preface to that volume, he may be supposed to have been born about 1667 or 1668. He was educated at Winchester, under William Harris, D. D., and seems to have remained there until about 1685, when he went to New College, Oxford, where he obtained a fellowship. He became B. A. in 1690, M. A. January 14th, 1692, and B. D. and D. D. 25th June, 1707.

record of its having been either set to music or performed having been discovered.

About the year 1690, the Rev. Samuel Wesley,
father of the celebrated John Wesley,* produced an ode
for St. Cecilia's day. This poem first appeared in print
in the *Gentleman's Journal* for April, 1694, with the
following remarks prefixed :—" I have here an Ode
" written some time since by Mr. Wesley, which has
" not been seen in Town, and so cannot well be said to
" want the charms of novelty. I am sure it has all the
" others that can be expected in a piece of that nature,
" and we might be apt to censure its ingenious author's
" resolution not to versifie any more, if any thing could
" be attempted in a poetic style, after the Life of Christ,
" with which Mr. Wesley has taken his leave of the
" Muses." Nothing has been found to show that this
ode was furnished with music anterior to the year 1794,

---

* Samuel Wesley, son of John Wesley of Whitchurch,
Dorsetshire, and grandson of Bartholomew Wesley, Minister
at Charmouth, in the same county, was born in 1662. He
was educated in the Free School of Dorchester under Henry
Dolling. In 1684, he became servitor at Exeter College,
Oxford. In the next year he published *Maggots, or Poems on
several subjects never before hanoled.* On 19th June, 1688, he
took the degree of B. A., and entering into holy orders,
obtained some curacy in or near London, and afterwards
became Rector of South Ormesby, Lincolnshire. In June,
1693, he published his heroic poem, *The Life of Our Blessed
Lord and Saviour Jesus Christ;* shortly after which he was presented to the living of Epworth, in Lincolnshire. He subsequently wrote other poetical pieces, and in 1723 obtained the
living of Wroot, Lincolnshire, which he held with Epworth
until his death on 30th April, 1735.

when, as already related in the account of the London celebrations, the author's grandson, Samuel Wesley, set it. If set, it was possibly performed at Oxford.

About 1692, Joseph Addison, then a demy of Magdalen College, wrote an ode, which was printed in 1694 in the fourth volume of *Miscellany Poems* published by Dryden, but the time and place of its performance and the name of the composer of the music are unrecorded. Festing's subsequent setting of this ode has been already noticed.

In 1693, an ode was written by Thomas Yalden, who was also a demy of Magdalen College,* and set to music by Daniel Purcell, then organist of the same College. The place of performance is not known, but from the circumstance of both poet and composer being of Magdalen College, it is not unlikely the ode may have been performed in the hall of that building. It was afterwards brought out in London and performed at Stationers' Hall, as appears by a memorandum on a manuscript score now in the library of Dr. Rimbault.

---

* Thomas Yalden (which name he adopted in lieu of his family name, Youlding) was born in Oxford, 2nd January, 1669-70. In 1688, he entered as a chorister of Magdalen College, in 1690 became demy, and in 1698 fellow. The latter of these appointments he resigned in 1713. He was the contemporary and friend of Addison and Sacheverell. Dr. Yalden held several ecclesiastical preferments and at the time of his death (16th July, 1736,) was Rector of Chalton and Clanfield, Hants, Preacher at Bridewell Hospital, and Prebendary of Chumleigh, Devon. Most of his poems are contained in Anderson's *Works of the British Poets.*

The poem was included in the fourth volume of Dryden's *Miscellany Poems,* 1694.

In 1696, " the Anniversary Meeting of the Lovers " of Musick on St. Cœcilia's Day" was held on the 27th November. The arrangements were under the charge of eight stewards, viz. :—" The Right Honour- " able The Lord Dunluce ; Sir John Smith, Baronet ; " John Hill, Esq. ; Colonel Henry Holt ; Colonel Na- " than Blackiston ; John Cary, Merchant ; Moses Snow, " B. M. ; and Nicola Matteis, Gent." As has been already noticed in the account of the London celebra- tion of this year, it is probable that an ode by Matteis was performed, and also that it was the same ode as had been produced in London. Divine service was celebrated at Christ Church, where a sermon was preached on the text, Colossians iii. 16, by Sampson Estwick, B.D. and Chaplain of Christ Church. This sermon was published in December, " at the request of " the Stewards," under the title of " The Usefulness " of Church-Musick." Of the preacher, who was an intimate friend of Dean Aldrich, Sir John Hawkins (*History of Music,* v. 14) has given the following in- teresting account :—" Sampson Estwick was one of the " first set of children [of the chapel-royal] after the " Restoration, and educated under Captain Henry " Cook. From the king's chapel he went to Oxford, " and entering in holy orders, became a chaplain of " Christ Church, where he was honoured with the " friendship of Dr. Aldrich * * * * Upon the de- " cease of Dr. Aldrich he came to London, and was " appointed one of the minor canons, and afterwards

" a cardinal of St. Paul's.* After he had been some
" time in the choir, he was presented to the rectory of
" St. Michael, Queenhithe, London. Nevertheless he
" continued to perform choral duty till near the time of
" his decease, when he was a little short of ninety
" years of age. In the former part of his life, viz.
" soon after his settlement in London, he was a candi-
" date for Gresham professor of music, but without
" success. He died in the month of February, 1739.
" In a character given of him in one of the public
" papers, he is styled a gentleman universally beloved
" for his exemplary piety and orthodox principles. This
" venerable servant of the church still survives in the
" remembrance of many persons now living. Bending
" beneath the weight of years, but preserving his facul-
" ties, and even his voice, which was a deep bass, till
" the last, he constantly attended his duty at St. Paul's,
" habited in a surplice; and with his bald head covered
" with a black satin coif, with gray hair round the edge
" of it, exhibited a figure the most awful that can well be
" conceived. Some compositions of his are extant, but
" not in print." Besides the appointments mentioned
by Hawkins, Estwick held that of Vicar of St. Helen's,
Bishopsgate. It is not improbable from the circumstance of Estwick's sermon having been preached at

---

* The cardinals are officers chosen from amongst the minor
canons, whose duty is to take notice of the absence or neglect
of the choir, and render an account thereof to the Dean and
Chapter. They take precedence next to the Sub Dean.
Formerly they had also other duties, which have fallen into
desuetude.

Christ Church, that that college may have been the place where the festival was this year held, and that its amiable and accomplished Dean, Dr. Henry Aldrich (eminent alike as a scholar, a divine, and a composer), may have presided upon the occasion.

In 1699 Addison furnished the devotees of music in Oxford with a second ode. The music for this was composed by Daniel Purcell, who, although he had no longer any official connexion with Oxford (having resigned his appointment as organist of Magdalen College in 1697), appears to have continued in great esteem there as a composer. His music for this ode has not been found.

In 1707, Daniel Purcell was again employed to compose an ode, but the name of his poetical coadjutor is not known, nor has either the poetry or the music been discovered. The ode was performed (as was also that produced in the ensuing year) at St. Mary Hall, " by Mr. Saunders and Mr. Court, assisted by the best " voices and hands."

The ode for 1708 was set to music by Dr. Blow, and was, in all probability, that eminent composer's latest production, his death happening on the 1st of October in this year. It is, on that account therefore, much to be regretted that we are unable to determine positively that one of the two manuscript compositions mentioned in the account of the London celebrations under the date of 1700, as being now in the possession of Dr. Rimbault, should be assigned to this year, and the more so, since there can be little, if any, doubt of its being the offering then made to the academic lovers of music.

Dr. Blow's ode for 1708 is the last of which any notice has been found as having been produced at Oxford on St. Cecilia's day. There is some reason, however, for supposing that the celebrations there continued until a later period, since we find that in 1713 a sermon was preached before the University at St. Mary's, on St. Cecilia's day, by William Dingley, B.D., Fellow of Corpus Christi College. This discourse, which was on Psalm civ. 33, 34, and had for its object the proving " Cathedral Music decent and useful," was shortly afterwards published with a dedication to Dr. Croft. This latter circumstance leads to a conjecture that Croft (who had this year obtained the degree of Doctor of Music,*) may have composed an ode for the occasion, notwithstanding no mention of such a production having yet been found.

About the year 1759 there was published in London music for " Mr. Pope's Ode on St. Cecilia's Day, com- " pos'd by William Walond, Bac. Mus. of Christ " Church College, Oxford." The writer has not been able to discover for what occasion this music was pro-

---

* Croft took this degree on 9th July, 1713, on which day the same distinction was also conferred on John Christopher Pepusch. Croft's exercise (two odes, one in English, the other in Latin, written by the Rev. Joseph Trapp in honour of the Peace of Utrecht, then just concluded,) was published in score under the name of *Musicus Apparatus Academicus.* Dr. Pepusch's exercise (which also celebrated the peace,) was not published. A copy of the words, printed on both sides of a folio leaf, is in the library of the Rev. Dr. Bliss, Principal of St. Mary Hall. Both exercises were performed in the Theatre, on Monday, July 13th.

duced, but from the circumstance of its being the only known composition of its author, coupled with the period of its publication, he conceives it to have been the exercise performed at Oxford on Walond's taking his bachelor's degree on July 5th, 1757. It is believed to be the first and only setting of Pope's ode in its original form. Of the composer, William Walond, but very few particulars can be gleaned. He was probably a native of Oxford, where he matriculated on June 25th, 1757, being described as "Gulielmus Walond, Organorum Pulsator;" whence we may suppose him to have been the organist, or assistant to the organist, of one of the churches or colleges there. About 1775 he became organist of Chichester Cathedral, which appointment he resigned in 1801. He resided in Chichester in extreme poverty and seclusion (subsisting on an annuity raised by the sale of some houses, and being rarely seen abroad,) until his death, which happened on 9th February, 1836. Walond appears to have had two sons; one of these, George, was admitted a chorister of Magdalen College on 13th April, 1768, and continued in that office until 1778; the other, Richard, matriculated at Christ Church, where he had probably been a chorister, on 14th July, 1770, being then sixteen years of age. On 24th March, 1775, he became one of the Clerks of Magdalen Collage, which office he retained until 1776, in which year (on 14th March,) he took the degree of B.A. as of New College. He subsequently became a vicar-choral of Hereford Cathedral.

Winchester.

At the commencement of the eighteenth century an annual musical celebration on St. Cecilia's day appears to have been customarily held in the city of Winchester, but the information obtained respecting it is exceedingly scanty.

In "A Collection of Songs compos'd by Vaughan Richardson," (a pupil of Blow, and for many years organist of Winchester Cathedral,) published in 1701, there is "A Song in praise of St. Cecilia," which was, no doubt, composed for and performed at the celebration at Winchester. A manuscript copy of this composition, differing in several points from the printed copy, is contained in a volume of manuscript music formerly belonging to Dr. Benjamin Cooke, and now in the library of the Sacred Harmonic Society.

The only other information concerning the Winchester celebrations is contained in the following advertisement which appeared in 1703. " The Annual Feast " for all Gentlemen and Ladies, Lovers of Musick, will " be held on the 22d of this instant November, at the " Bishop of Winchester's Palace called Woolsey, near " Winchester,* where (in honour of St. Cecilia,) will " be performed a new set of Vocal and Instrumental

---

* At this time the see of Winchester was filled by Bishop Mews. The episcopal palace at Wolvesey (mentioned in the advertisement,) was begun by Bishop Morley in 1684, and completed by Bishop Trelawney, who held the see from 1707 to 1721. Having fallen to decay, the greater part of it was taken down between forty and fifty years ago, the present episcopal residence being formed out of the west wing.

" Musick, compos'd by Mr. Vaughan Richardson, Or-
" ganist of Winchester Cathedral. Tickets, 2s. 6d.
" each, may be had at Mr. Colson's, Mr. Williams's,
" Mr. Gosnell's, and Mr. Richardson's in Winchester."

Salisbury.

In the early part of the last century a " Society of
" Lovers of Musick " existed at Salisbury. The earliest memorial of the proceedings of this body is to be
found in " A Sermon Preached at the Cathedral Church
" of Sarum, November the 30th, 1727, Being the
" Anniversary day appointed for the Meeting of the
" Society of Lovers of Musick. By Thomas Naish,
" M.A. Sub Dean of Sarum." A passage in the preface to this discourse shows the meetings to have been
held for some time previously, and to have been well
supported. It also appears that at these meetings music
was made ancillary to charity. The objects of the
charity are not named, but inasmuch as three of the
eight stewards of the Society appointed for conducting
the festival of 1727 were clergymen, it seems likely
that the profits of the meeting were applied to some
such purpose as those of the Meetings of the three
Choirs of Gloucester, Worcester, and Hereford.* The
Stewards of the meeting in 1727 were " Sir George
" Hamsom Kt. and Bar. The Rev. Mr. Richard

---

* There were at this time in Wiltshire two charitable
foundations for the residence and support of clergymen's
widows, viz., Bishop Ward's hospital at Salisbury founded in
1683, for ten inmates, and that founded at Froxfield in 1686
by the Duchess of Somerset for fifteen widows.

" Younger, The Rev. Mr. Peter Hersent, The Rev.
" Mr. John Talman, Thomas Hasket, Esq., Edmund
" Pitman, Esq., John Clark, Esq., and John Long,
" Esq." It is supposed that a performance of secular
music took place after the Church service, in the same
manner as in London.

No notices of the meetings for the period intervening
between 1727 and 1741 have come to the writer's
knowledge, although it is most likely that the meeting
was regularly continued. In November, 1741, it was
advertised in these terms: " Salisbury. St. Cecilia's
" Concert will be perform'd this year at the Assembly
" House in New Street on Friday the 27th instant.
" There will be Vocal and Instrumental Musick at the
" Cathedral Church in the Morning, and an Ordinary
" for Gentlemen at the Crown and Mitre Tavern.
" N.B. There will be several additional performers
" from Oxford and Bath, and a Ball after the Concert.
" The Subscription Concert which in course falls on
" Thursday the 26th, will be put off till Saturday the
" 28th. Tickets for St. Cecilia's Concert may be had
" at 2s. 6d. each from the City Musick, and at Mr.
" Westley's Coffee House in Silver Street."

In 1742, " The Festival of St. Cecilia," was announced for celebration, " as usual," on Thursday, 25th
November, " for the benefit of the City Musick." The
performance at the cathedral consisted of Handel's
Te Deum and Jubilate (composed for the Thanksgiving
for the Peace of Utrecht,) and two of his anthems ; the
orchestra being strengthened by a reinforcement of
" additional hands from London, Oxford, and Bath."

The "Ordinary for the Gentlemen" was given at the Three Lions.

In 1743, the meeting (still announced as "The Festival of St. Cecilia,") took place on 20th October, the proceeds being appropriated "for the benefit of the City "Musick and the poor Widow Gingell." The latter was probably the widow of Richard Gingell, whose name had appeared in the advertisements of the preceding year as one of those from whom tickets were to be obtained, but who was not mentioned in this year's announcement. The additional performers for this festival were brought from Bristol, Oxford, and Bath.

In 1744, the festival was held on Thursday, 25th October, "for the benefit of the Town Musick."

No notice has been found of any festival in the following year, and it is probable that the agitation and excitement occasioned by the Scottish rebellion prevented any being held.

In 1746, however, the festival was again celebrated, the meeting taking place on Thursday, 17th October, and "the Town Musick" again receiving the benefit. "Mr. Handel's New Te Deum" (that produced on occasion of the victory at Dettingen in 1743,) was introduced at the cathedral at this meeting.

Of the meeting in 1747 no trace has been discovered.

In the following year (1748) an important change was made in the constitution of the festival by the extension of the meeting to two days. It will have been observed that after 1742 an alteration had taken place in the time of holding the annual meeting, which, instead of being, as formerly, on some day in November nigh to St. Cecilia's day, had been shifted to the month of October. By the further change now introduced, more of the character of the modern musical festival than of the old " Festival of St. Cecilia " was imparted to the meeting, although the latter title still continued to be made use of, and an ode in praise of music still formed part of the performances. The festival this year was celebrated on 19th and 20th October. There was " different musick each day at the Cathedral Church," and each evening a concert and ball at the Assembly Room in New Street; Handel's music to Alexander's Feast being performed on one evening, and his Acis and Galatea on the other. " The best voices and " hands from Oxford, Bath, and elsewhere " were employed in the performance. The ordinary was probably discontinued, as the announcements in this and subsequent years are silent respecting it.

In 1749, the time of holding the festival was again changed, and the meeting took place on the 19th and 20th September. The performances at the Cathedral included " each day one of Mr. Handel's Grand Te " Deums, and two of his most celebrated Anthems." The first evening's concert at the Assembly House consisted of " the whole of the Pastoral Masque of Acis " and Galatea." On the next evening was produced what was no doubt regarded by many of the good folks of Sarum as the most striking and interesting feature of the festival, viz., " The Grand New Overture and " Musick compos'd by Mr. Handel for the Royal Fire- " works " exhibited in London on occasion of the rejoicings for the Peace of Aix-la-Chapelle. A duet

from Judas Maccabeus,* and " a Grand Concerto
" for a Trumpet, Kettle Drums, &c. " constituted the
remainder of the first part of the concert, the second
part consisting of " the celebrated Ode written by Mr.
" Dryden for St. Cecilia's Day, and set to Musick by
" Mr. Handel." Each evening's concert was followed
by a ball. The usual assistance for (what the advertisements term) " this great performance " was obtained " from Oxford, Bath, and other places."

In 1750, a closer approach to the character of the
present musical festival was made by the introduction
of an entire oratorio at one of the evening concerts.
The following account of this year's performances appears in the *Salisbury Journal* of October 8th.   " On
" the 4th and 5th of this Month was celebrated in this
" City, the Musical Festival of St. Cecilia.   There were
" performed each day in the Morning at the Cathedral
" Church a Te Deum of Mr. Handel and Two of his
" Anthems by above Thirty performers, Vocal and
" Instrumental.   At the New Assembly Room on the
" first Night was performed the Messiah, or Sacred
" Oratorio,† and on the second Night L'Allegro Il

---

* The popularity acquired by this oratorio on its production appears to have been by no means confined to the metropolis.   In September, 1748, a musical professor in Salisbury
announced as the most attractive features of his benefit concert,
" the two celebrated French Horns from the Opera House;
" And likewise the famous March in Judas Maccabeus,
" Accompanied by the Original Side Drum."

† This is an early instance of the performance of this great
work in the provinces.   It was not performed at the Meetings
of the Three Choirs until 1757.

H

" Penseroso, both set to Music by the same great Com-
" poser. Among the Voices were Dr. Hayes, Professor
" of Music at Oxford, and Signor Guadagni, a cele-
" brated Italian. The Music as well at the Church as
" at the Assembly Room was performed with great
" Exactness throughout, and in many parts with great
" Elegance. There was a very laudable Attention on
" the Part of the Audience, which was very numerous.*
" Above four hundred Persons were present each Night
" at the Assembly Room, in which number were in-
" cluded the principal Nobility and Gentry within many
" miles of this place." In the advertisements of the
Festival " a Song for St. Cecilia's Day by Dryden "
was announced to follow Milton's Allegro and Penseroso, on the second night. This, however, appears to
have been laid aside in favour of Il Moderato, which,
according to the book of words, formed the third part
of the second night's performance. A new organ was
opened at this festival in the Assembly Room, which
edifice had probably been rebuilt, as both in the announcements and the newspaper account it is designated
" The New Assembly Room." A ball " for the ladies "
followed each evening's concert " as usual ; " an entertainment which would now-a-days be regarded as a
very extraordinary, not to say unseemly, appendage to
a performance of the Messiah.

The festival was now become an object of great atten-

---

* Are we to infer from this statement that the audiences of
the day were accustomed to treat music as merely an agreeable accompaniment to conversation ?

tion. In 1751 it was heralded by the following paragraph in the *Salisbury Journal* of 23rd September:—
" We hear a great deal of Company will be here on
" Thursday and Friday next at the Festival of St. Ce-
" cilia." In the next week the same paper gave the
following account of the performance:—" The Anniver-
" sary Festival of Music was celebrated here on the 26th
" and 27th instant. The performance in the Church
" on the first day consisted of Mr. Handel's Te Deum
" compos'd for Duke Chandos,* and two of his cele-
" brated Coronation Anthems. On the second day his
" Te Deum compos'd for his present Majesty,† toge-
" ther with the remaining two Coronation Anthems.
" At the Assembly Room on the first evening was per-
" formed Alexander's Feast; on the second the Ora-
" torio of Samson, both set to Music by the same great
" Composer. The performers were more than Forty
" in number, among which were several as well vocal
" as instrumental from Oxford, Bath, and London.
" The Performance itself was accurate and just (there
" being scarce an Error throughout the Whole,) and
" met with general approbation from a very polite and
" numerous audience. Among whom were * * *
" most of the best families within many miles of this
" place to the amount of more than three hundred per-
" sons the first night and near as many the second."

---

* Handel wrote two Te Deums for this nobleman's chapel,
one in the key of A and the other in that of B flat.

† By this the Dettingen Te Deum must have been intended.

The celebration in the next year (1752) furnishes one of the earliest instances in this country of the performance of oratorios in churches; the caution exhibited in describing the work being very remarkable.* The account of the performances given in the *Salisbury Journal* is very interesting, and is as follows :—
" Salisbury, September 30. The Anniversary Musical
" Festival was celebrated here on the 27th and 28th
" instant. The Musick in the Cathedral Church on
" the first day began with an Overture,† then followed
" a Te Deum set for Voices and Instruments, then an
" Anthem taken from the first and second Acts of the
" Messiah or Sacred Oratorio ; and at the conclusion
" of the Service the famous Coronation Anthem of God
" save the King.‡ On the second day a different
" Overture, the same Te Deum, an Anthem from the
" third Act of the Messiah or Sacred Oratorio ; the
" conclusion as before, God save the King. At the
" Assembly Room on the first night was performed
" Samson, on the second, Judas Maccabeus, both of

---

* Handel's Messiah was not performed in the Cathedrals at the Meetings of the Three Choirs until 1759, when it was introduced into the morning performances at Hereford. It was first performed in Worcester Cathedral in 1761, but was not given in Gloucester Cathedral until 1769. No other oratorios were performed in the churches at these meetings until after 1784.

† This is the first mention which occurs of the introduction of purely instrumental pieces into the church at these celebrations.

‡ The last movement of Handel's anthem, Zadok the Priest, is here intended.

" them Oratorios of the greatest merit. All the above
" mentioned pieces were the compositions of one and
" the same Author, Mr. Handel, whose fertile and
" transcendant genius has justly acquired him a con-
" tinued and universal Admiration for more than forty
" years past. The vocal performers were eighteen in
" number, among whom the principal were Dr. Hayes,
" Professor of Musick at Oxford, his two Sons, and
" Mr. Freeman. The Instrumental Performers con-
" sisted of sixteen Violins, two Hautboys, Two Tenor
" Violins, a Bassoon, a Harpsichord, Four Violoncellos,
" Two Double Bases, with French Horns, Trumpets
" and Drums. The Music was performed with great
" Spirit and exactness, and was received with Applause
" by a numerous and brilliant audience."

In 1753 the festival was held on the 19th and 20th
September, and again all the music was selected from
the works of Handel. The performances at the Cathedral included the overtures to Saul and the Occasional
Oratorio, different Te Deums, and the four Coronation
Anthems. L'Allegro was performed at the first, and
Judas Maccabeus at the second of the evening concerts.
" Between the Acts Mr. Gordon entertained the Com-
" pany with an elegant performance on the Violoncello,
" and Mr. Millar with another on the Bassoon." The
orchestra consisted of between forty and fifty performers.
There was present " the greatest appearance of Nobility
" and Gentry ever known upon the like occasion, the
" number in the Assembly Room being upwards of four
" hundred the first night and between three and four
" hundred the second night."

And here will we terminate the account of the musical celebrations in Salisbury. It will have been observed that, although these annual performances continued to be announced under the name of " St. Cecilia's Festival," they had gradually assumed a character altogether distinct from the celebrations on St. Cecilia's day out of which they originally sprung. Any account, therefore, of their further progress would (however interesting in itself,) be foreign to the purpose of the present work. Having, however, entered so much at length into the history of these early musical festivals at Salisbury, it may perhaps be not altogether out of place to allude to the circumstance of their having entirely escaped the researches of Mr. Crosse, when engaged upon the interesting " Sketch of the Rise and Progress of Musical " Festivals in Great Britain," prefixed to his valuable *Account of the York Musical Festival*, 1823. The earliest Salisbury Festival mentioned by Mr. Crosse is that held in 1789.

Devizes.

In the year 1749 " a grand performance of Vocal " and Instrumental Musick," to which the title of " St. " Cecilia's Festival" was given, took place in the town of Devizes, the undertakers being probably influenced by the success attendant on the Cecilian Festivals held at Salisbury. This festival was celebrated on Wednesday, 11th October, being (according to the announcement) " the last day of the Green Fair." Purcell's Te Deum and Jubilate and three of Handel's anthems were performed at St. John's Church in the morning,

" with Voices and Instruments, by the Assistance of
" divers of the most eminent performers from Salisbury,
" Bath and other places." In the evening there was
a Concert and Ball at the Town Hall. The tickets
were (as at Winchester and Salisbury) 2s. 6d. each.*
In 1750 similar performances were given on Tuesday
and Wednesday, 25th and 26th September, but the
title of " St. Cecilia's Festival" was dropped. On this
occasion performers were brought from London as well
as from Bath and Salisbury. We are told that " Signor
" Guadagni's most excellent singing together with the
" elegant performance of several of the most eminent
" hands who came from London on purpose to assist,
" was most justly admir'd." The performance gave
such general satisfaction that a subscription was entered
into for a similar meeting in the ensuing year, and we
accordingly find performances announced for 10th and
11th October, 1751, the title of " St. Cecilia's Festival"
being however still disused.

---

* This appears to have been for many years the usual price
of concert tickets in the provinces. Hearne, in his *Diary*,
speaks in terms of reprobation of Handel's charge of 5s. for
admission to his performances at Oxford in July, 1733. It
must not, however, be forgotten that Handel's being a German
and an adherent of the house of Hanover must have rendered
him peculiarly obnoxious to the learned antiquary, who was
a staunch Jacobite.

CHAPTER V.

Celebrations in Scotland and Ireland.

Edinburgh.

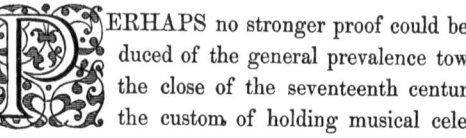 ERHAPS no stronger proof could be ad-
duced of the general prevalence towards
the close of the seventeenth century of
the custom of holding musical celebra-
tions on St. Cecilia's day than the fact that such custom
extended to the northern metropolis.

The means of information as to the Edinburgh celebrations are exceedingly limited, consisting, in fact, of
one document only, from which it appears that the
manner of these celebrations was widely different from
that in use in England, the performances being confined
almost exclusively (for reasons, probably, not difficult
to surmise,) to instrumental music. A copy of this
document is contained in a paper by W. Tytler of
Woodhouselee, Esq., " On the fashionable amusements
" and entertainments in Edinburgh in the last century ;"
printed in the *Transactions of the Society of Antiqua-*
ries of Scotland, vol. I. 1792. It is entitled " The
" Order of the Instrumental Music for the Feast of St.
" Cecilia, 22nd November, 1695 ;" and gives a list of
the pieces performed, and of the names of the per-

formers. The former comprised " Clerk's Overture," Sonatas by Corelli, Bassani, Torelli, Finger, Barrett, and Pepulsh,* two solos by unnamed composers, and three chorusses. Of these last neither the initial words nor the composers' names are mentioned, but from a note affixed it is inferred that a motett by Bassani was included amongst them. The performers (that is, the instrumentalists, for no vocalists are included in the list,) numbered thirty; nineteen being amateurs, gentlemen of rank and fashion, and the remaining eleven professors. The most noticable of the latter were Daniel Thomson, a celebrated performer on the trumpet (distinguished for his style of executing Purcell's trumpet pieces), the father of William Thomson, the editor of the collection of Scots songs entitled *Orpheus Caledonius;* and Adam Craig, a violinist, who in 1730 published a collection of Scottish tunes. The place of performance is not mentioned, neither is there anything to indicate whether the celebration was an isolated one, or part of a series.

When we consider the austerity which then characterized the Scottish people, and the strong dislike (verging nearly to abhorrence,) which they evinced towards dramatic performances, assemblies, balls, and

---

* Guiseppe Torelli was a native of Verona, and a famous violinist. In 1703 he was concert master at Anspach, and subsequently maestro di capella of San Petronio at Bologna. His compositions for instruments were in high esteem. John Barrett, a pupil of Dr. Blow, was music master at Christ's Hospital, and organist of St. Mary at Hill, London. " Pepulsh" is probably a misprint for Pepusch.

ındeed nearly every species of amusement, it is matter of surprise that the celebrations on St. Cecilia's day should have taken place without provoking some hostile manifestation. That no such opposition was offered may be accounted for by the supposition that the celebrations were held privately, instead of, as in other places, assuming a public character, and were therefore, if not tolerated, at least regarded with indifference by the general public.

Dublin.

In the early part of the eighteenth century a Musical Society was established in Dublin, amongst the founders of which are said to have been Dr. Benjamin Pratt, Provost of Trinity College from 1710 to 1717 ; Thomas Rosingrave, Organist of St. Patrick's Cathedral, Arthur Dawson, afterwards Baron of the Exchequer, Garret Wellesley (grandfather of the late Duke of Wellington), Kane O'Hara, the dramatist, and Laurence Whyte, an excellent mathematician and author of some poems. This Society gave an annual concert on St. Cecilia's day in St. Patrick's Cathedral. The earliest allusion to these performances which has been discovered is contained in the following lines by Dean Swift, written probably about 1724 or 1725.

" DR. SWIFT TO HIMSELF ON ST. CECILIA'S DAY.

" Grave Dean of St. Patrick's, how comes it to pass,
" That you, who know music no more than an ass,
" That you, who so lately were writing of Drapiers,*

---

* The celebrated Letters of " M. B., Drapier, Dublin," appeared in 1723.

" Should lend your Cathedral to players and scrapers ?
" To act such an opera once in a year,
" So offensive to ev'ry true Protestant ear,
" With trumpets, and fiddles, and organs, and singing,
" Will sure the Pretender and Popery bring in.
" No Protestant prelate, His Lordship, or Grace,
" Durst there show his Right or Most Reverend face :
" How would it pollute their crosiers and rochets,
" To listen to minims, and quavers, and crotchets ?

" The rest is wanting."

The musical portion of the celebration which was, as
we see by the above lines, accompanied by an orchestra,
was most likely, as in England, composed of the Te
Deum and Jubilate and some anthems.   The following
announcement (made by a handbill,) would, however,
seem to warrant an inference that an ode was also performed on these occasions.   " The Power of Music, a
" Song in honour of St. Cecilia's Day.   Occasionally
" published on the grand assembly of the Musical So-
" ciety at St. Patrick's Church, this twenty-third day
" of November, 1730.   Dublin, Printed by Richard
" Dickson, and sold at the Globe Coffee House on Essex
" Bridge, 1730."   The title, " The Power of Music,"
would seem to indicate Dryden's " Alexander's Feast,"
as the " Song " thus announced.

A sermon was, no doubt, preached at each of these
meetings, but one only of these discourses has come to
the writer's knowledge.   This was preached at St. Patrick's Cathedral on St. Cecilia's day, 1731, by Dr.
Thomas Sheridan, the intimate friend and associate of
Swift, and an ardent lover of music.   It has for its
text, Psalm xxiii. 1, 2, 3, and 4, and is in defence of

the employment of music in the service of the church.
It was printed at Dublin soon after its delivery " by
" S. Powell in Crane Lane, for the Author,"* with
a dedication " To the Honourable Musical Society,"
whom the author describes in the preface as " that
" numerous and honourable Society lately instituted for
" the improvement of music in Churches and other
" solemn performances." He further says that he pub-
lishes the sermon in consequence of a report " from se-
" veral quarters that the Sermon which I preached in the
" Cathedral of St. Patrick's on last St. Cecilia's day had
" given offence to many dissenters," and that he " was
" accused of delivering Popish doctrines." What
ground of complaint the dissenters had, let the reader
judge from the following extracts from the sermon. In
one place the preacher says, " Some Christian Thracians
" among us are for breaking the strings of David's
" harp, and pulling down our organ, although, at the
" same time, they keep up psalm-singing in their con-
" venticles, for no other visible reason but because one
" is an appointment of the Church, and the other is a
" creature of their own ; preferring their own untuned
" voices to the regular methods of a decent choir."
Again, he introduces a declamation against voluntaries,
which he defines to be, " what the organist pleases to
" run off his fingers without any regard whether melody
" or harmony be in it; nothing but a discomposed
" rhapsody of his own raving imagination, which must

---

* A copy is preserved in the library of Trinity College,
Dublin.

" be highly offensive to any person who has judgment
" enough to be tormented with its faults." And adds,
" It is too like extempore prayer, and that is saying
" enough." The publication of this sermon evoked a
reply in the form of " A Letter to the Rev. Thomas
" Sheridan, occasioned by a Sermon preached in St.
" Patrick's Church on St. Cecilia's Day. To which is
" added the History of St. Cecilia." The writer's
arguments are directed against the use of instrumental
music in Church service, and against the celebration of
any day in honour of St. Cecilia. No effect, however,
would seem to have been produced by this letter, since
St. Cecilia's day was kept in the following year with
greater ceremony than ever. " Mr. Purcell's Te Deum
" and Corelli's Concerto were performed, and a sermon
" suitable was preached by Mr. Sheridan. The same
" night the Rt. Hon. Visc. Mountjoy gave a ball to
" several ladies at Taylor's Hall." (Carson's *Weekly
Journal.*)

The foregoing are all the particulars that it has been
found possible to collect relative to the musical celebrations on St. Cecilia's day in Dublin. In a volume of
Miscellaneous Poems, edited by Matthew Concanen, and
published in London in 1724, is an Ode for St. Cecilia's
day, entitled " Saul dispossess'd," written by Mr. J. B.
Most of the pieces in this volume being by Irish writers
and on Irish subjects, renders it probable that this ode
may have been produced at one of the Dublin celebrations. What author concealed himself under the
initials " J. B." is unknown. His production is in

manner, form, and language a close parody of Dryden's Alexander's Feast.

Such is the history of the musical celebrations on St. Cecilia's day in Great Britain; an account which, it is hoped, will not be deemed either unacceptable or uninteresting by the musical reader. Established at a period when a general depravity pervaded nearly every class of the community—when the evil example of a dissolute and profligate monarch and a licentious and abandoned aristocracy exerted a baneful influence over all within its reach—when in the public theatre indecency usurped the place of wit—when the sister arts of poetry and music were commonly perverted to the basest of uses, and the greatest poets and musicians of the time, yielding to the general corruption, united with their meaner brethren in the debasement and degradation of those noble arts;—these celebrations present a pleasing and striking contrast to the generality of the objects by which they are surrounded. The promoters of them appear to have been influenced solely by a pure and disinterested love of the musical art, and those engaged in carrying out the design, both poets and musicians, to have entered upon and executed their tasks in a laudable spirit of emulation. To the Cecilian poets a high meed of approbation is due for the worthy manner in which they performed their work. Their avoidance of allusions to passing political events has been before incidentally noticed; but a still higher praise belongs to them;—that of withstanding the temptation of making their poetry acceptable by descending to gratify the vile taste of the times. Their verses are sometimes puerile, often dull and prosaic, but never vicious.

Of the beneficial influence of these celebrations in promoting the taste for, and cultivation of the higher branches of musical art, there can be no doubt. That they were instrumental in the diffusion of a taste for music, we have ample testimony in the numerous provincial festivals which sprung up in imitation of them, and of which those recorded in this work were probably only a portion. A more diligent cultivation of the art was a natural consequence of the establishment of a festival, which, on each successive annual recurrence, required the writing, composition, and production of a new work, and thereby engendered and kept alive a spirit of generous rivalry in both poets and composers.

The claim of these celebrations to be considered the source of the modern musical festivals seems undeniable. The origin of such festivals is generally ascribed to the Meetings of the Three Choirs of Gloucester, Worcester, and Hereford, which, in their turn, are supposed to have been suggested by the Anniversary Festivals of the Sons of the Clergy. These latter were held as early as the middle of the seventeenth century, but it was not until near its close, and perhaps not until early in the following century, that the performance of the musical portion of Divine service by a large choir, aided by an instrumental band, was first made a prominent and attractive feature of them. As such a mode of performing service had been customary at the Cecilian festivals for several years prior to its introduction at those of the Sons of the Clergy, no doubt can remain that the practice of the " Musical Society" was adopted by the elder body. We may thus trace the modern musical festival back to the musical celebrations on St. Cecilia's day. It is interesting also to observe, that the form of the musical festival does not essentially differ from that of the Cecilian celebrations. The morning performances, confined to Church service, oratorios, or other sacred music (in many places performed in a sacred edifice,) are clearly derived from the Church service of the earlier institution ; whilst an equally strong resemblance exists between the evening performances of secular music and the afternoon performance of the Cecilian ode.

CHAPTER VI.

Continental Celebrations.

France.

IN a relation of the musical solemnizations of St. Cecilia's day on the continent of Europe, those of France are on many accounts entitled to the first claim on our attention. The earliest mention of St. Cecilia with which we are acquainted is made by a French historian; the earliest religious service on the anniversary of the Saint's martyrdom appears in a French ritual; and the first recorded instance of any solemnity on St. Cecilia's day having in view the advancement of the art of music was held in a French city. Of the latter we are fortunately in possession of ample details, and as these are not only interesting in themselves as connected with the subject of this work, but also as bringing under notice the names of many musical composers not otherwise known to us, and still more, as the institution to which they relate is not mentioned by any musical or other writer, a larger space is devoted to them than would otherwise have been deemed necessary.

The celebration spoken of is that which has been

before named as established at Evreux, a city of Normandy, in the year 1571.

At that time an association, consisting of persons
connected with the Cathedral of Notre Dame at Evreux
and some of the principal inhabitants of the city, was
formed for the purpose of establishing, by means of
voluntary donations and subscriptions, and with the
concurrence of the Dean and Chapter of the Cathedral,
a service " in honour of God, under the invocation of
" St. Cecilia, in the Cathedral Church of Our Lady at
" Evreux, on the Feast day of the said Saint, in each
" year to come for ever."

The founders were twenty-one in number, and
amongst them were the following members of the Cathedral, viz. Robert Feret, canon, Jehan Du Buz,
organist, Jehan Jourdain, master of the children of the
choir, Jehan Boette, Jehan Berthault, Mauxe Challumeau, and Oliver Challumeau, chaplains, and Eustache
La Flament, succentor; the principal lay members being Robert Gueriboult, Visconte de Conches et Brétheuil, Louis Le Mercié, Visconte d'Evreux, Jehan
de la Rocque, President of the Court of Aids of Normandy, Guillaume Costeley, organist and valet de
chambre to the king (Charles IX.),* and Robert
Motte, a singer in the king's chapel.

The service consisted of a solemn celebration of ves-

---

* Costeley (who was of Scotch parentage) was born in 1531.
He was the author of a treatise on Music published at Paris
in 1579. Some Chansons of his composition are contained in
a collection of *Chansons à quatre et à cinq parties*, published by
Adrian Le Roi and Robert Ballard in 1567.

pers and complin on the vigil of St. Cecilia, high mass,
vespers, and complin on the festival, and a requiem
mass for the repose of the souls of departed founders on
the morrow.

The foundation was distinguished by the title of " Le
" Puy de Musique."

By the laws of the association the members were
required every year to elect one of their body as Prince,
or Master of the festival for the ensuing year. The
duties of this officer were to take charge of the general
arrangements of the festival ; to provide (at the cost of
the association) the necessary tapestries, candles, chap-
lets of flowers, &c. for the decoration of the church and
the image of St. Cecilia on the feast day ; and to cause
to be prepared in a fit place (after mass on the feast
day) a table for the confraternity and company to dine
at ; the charges of which entertainment it was provided
should be borne by the founders, the Prince not being
obliged to contribute anything unless it so pleased him ;
an exemption which induced most of those who were
elected to fill the office of Prince to seek to testify their
regard for the institution by not only taking upon themselves the entire cost of the entertainment, but by vying
with each other in a display of liberality and profusion
on the occasion. Once in every three years a treasurer
was to be elected. To this officer pertained (amongst
other things) the charge of the coffer made for the
preservation of the papers and books of the foundation.
After mass on St. Cecilia's day he was to distribute
twenty-five sols in alms to poor persons.

The annals of the foundation are as follows.

A. D. 1571.—Guillaume Costeley, the king's organist, was the first Prince of the association. The feast was held in his house of Moullin de la Planche, and he contributed to the funds a donation of ten livres.

A. D. 1572.—Robert Gueriboult, Visconte de Conches et Brétheuil, was chosen Prince. The feast was held at his house, opposite St. Nicholas' Church, where he entertained the company at dinner and supper on the feast day, and at breakfast the next day at his own expense. He had in the preceding year made a donation of twenty livres to the funds of the association. Jehan Jourdain, master of the children of the choir, one of the founders, died during the year, and was succeeded in his office by Jehan Boette, also a member of the association. Four new members were admitted this year,—Jehan Du Pray, canon, and Jehan Le Tellier, chaplain of the cathedral; Jehan Le Doulx, President au siége presidial d'Evreux, and Etienne Michel, cure de Croissy.

A. D. 1573.—A further increase took place in the number of members;—Guy de Limoges, abbot of Lisle Dieu, and canon of the cathedral; Raoul Boullenc, Sieur de Blanfosse and treasurer of the cathedral, and his brother, Jaques, Sieur d'Angerville la Riviere; Robert Dagommer, canon, and Nicolas Le Bel, precentor and chaplain of the cathedral, being added to the list,—all of whom contributed liberally to the funds. An agreement was entered into with the Dean and Chapter of Evreux, by which that body, in consideration

of a payment of twenty-eight livres, granted a perpetual
rent-charge of eight livres (secured on the cathedral
revenues), to be paid annually, in certain specified pro-
portions, to the canon, deacon, subdeacon, clerks, choristers, organist, and others engaged in the performance
of the church services on the vigil, feast day, and morrow
of St. Cecilia. In this agreement, which bears date
Monday 12th October, 1573, the nature of the services
and the particular psalms, motetts, &c. to be performed
at each are clearly defined and specified. The Prince
of the year was Jehan de la Rocque, President of the
Court of Aids of Normandy. The feast was held at
the Deanery.

A. D. 1574.—Guy de Limoges, abbot of Lisle Dieu
and canon of the cathedral was chosen Prince. He
kept the feast at his own charges in a very liberal
manner at the Deanery. Three new members were
this year admitted into the confraternity.

A. D. 1575.—This year witnessed a most important
extension of the plan of the festival by the institution
of prizes for the best sacred and secular compositions.
These prizes were seven in number, and were as follows:—for the best Latin motett of five parts and two
overtures, the words being in honour of God, or in
praise of St. Cecilia, a silver organ:—for the next best
motett, a silver harp:—for the best chanson of five
parts, a silver lute, and for the next best a silver lyre:—
for the most agreeable air of four parts, a silver cornet:
—for the best chanson of four parts, a silver flute; and

for the most excellent French sonnet with two overtures, the Triumph of St. Cecilia, enriched with gold, which was the greatest prize. Each prize bore a suitable motto and inscription. For the purpose of inviting the competition of the best musicians, as well foreign as native, for these prizes, it was ordained that the Prince and Treasurer should annually cause to be printed " by " Adrian Le Roy, printer of music to the king, dwell- " ing at the sign of Mount Parnassus, in Mount St. " Hilaire, in Paris," two hundred *affiches*, which were to be distributed in divers places three months at least before the festival. The prizes (the form and fashion of which were to be approved by the founders) were directed to be obtained from " Jehan Laurens, gold- " smith, dwelling in Paris, on the Pont au Change, at " the sign of the Mill." The compositions sent in to compete for the prizes were to be received and regis- tered by the Master of the children of the choir. The brethren of the foundation were to elect a Dean of the " Puy," by whom, in conjunction with a number of the founders possessed of a competent musical knowledge, the competing compositions (which were to be sung by the choir of the cathedral) were to be judged. After the decision, the Prince, founders, and brethren were to proceed, accompanied by the choir, to the grand en- trance of the cathedral, and there, after returning thanks to God for the success of their enterprise, to sing the prize motetts, and publish the names of the authors. Thence returning to the house of the children of the choir, the prize chansons, air, and sonnet were to be performed, and the authors' names proclaimed in like manner. After this the company were to sit down to a plain supper in the same place. The Master of the children of the choir was enjoined to enter the prize compositions, with the names of the authors, in five books to be provided for that purpose. The Prince for the year 1575 was Louis Le Mercié, Visconte d'Evreux, who entertained the brethren and company very handsomely at his house in the parish of St. Thomas. The prizes were awarded to the following composers :—the organ to the famous Orlando de Lasso, then chapel master to the Duke of Bavaria ; the harp to Raymond de la Cassaigne, Master of the children of Notre Dame at Paris ; the lute to Jacques Salmon of Picardy, singer and valet de chambre to the king (Henry III.) ;* the lyre to Nicolas Millot, one of the gentlemen of the king's chapel ; the cornet to Eustache du Caurroy, one of the singers in the king's chapel ;† and the Triumph to one

---

* Salmon was also violinist and composer to the king. He composed, conjointly with Beaulieu, another French musician, music for a "Ballet comique de la Royne," performed in 1581, on occasion of the nuptials of the Duke de Joyeuse with the queen's sister. A specimen of the music of this ballet is given by Dr. Burney in his *History of Music*, iii. 279. Salmon resided in Paris during the latter half of the sixteenth century.

† François Eustache du Caurroy, born in 1549, was one of the most celebrated musicians of his time, being called by his contemporaries the prince of musicians. He was destined by his father to enter the order of Malta, in which an elder brother had become a commander ; but devoting himself to music and acquiring a great reputation, his father was induced to abandon his design. Entering into holy orders, he became canon of the Holy Chapel at Paris, and Prior of St.

of the members of the association, Jehan Boette, master
of the choristers of Evreux Cathedral. The flute does
not appear to have been given this year. No new
members were added to the fraternity.

A. D. 1576.—St. Cecilia's day falling this year on a
Saturday, the celebration was, by permission of the
Bishop and Dean and Chapter of Evreux, deferred until
the next day (Sunday), when it was held in the cathedral. Raoul Boullenc, Sieur de Blanfosse and Treasurer
of the Cathedral, filled the office of Prince this year and
entertained the company at his canonal house. The
festival was held, by permission of the chapter, in the
house of the children of the choir. The ordinary choir
was this year assisted by Jacques Preston of Flanders,
an excellent bass singer attached to the establishment
of M. de Braban, Abbé de Vallemont, and by Claude
Le Painctre, Master and Conductor of the chapel of
M. de Villeroy. Le Painctre gained the prize (the
silver flute) for the best chanson of four parts. The
other prizes were adjudged to Eustache du Caurroy,
who had in the previous year received the cornet, and

Aioul de Provins. He was royal chapel master for nearly
forty years, serving successively Francis II., Charles IX.,
Henry III., and Henry IV. The place of superintendent of
the king's music was created for him in 1599. He died 7th
August, 1609, and was buried in the Great Augustine Church,
where his successor, Nicolas Formè, erected a tomb to his
memory. This tomb was destroyed in the revolution of 1789.
A Christmas carol of du Caurroy's composition may be seen
in Burney's *History of Music,* iii. 285.

this year obtained the organ; to Georges de la Hele, master of the choristers at Tournay, who carried off both the harp and the lute;* to Claude Petit-Jan, master of the choristers of Verdun cathedral, who gained the lyre; to Frabizio Cajetan, an Italian singer belonging to the chapel of Monsignor de Guyse, who received the cornet; and to Barillault, one of the suite of M. de Rouville, to whom the Triumph was awarded. Four new members, all ecclesiastics, were admitted at this festival.

A. D. 1577.—Jehan Ledoulx, President au siege presidial, was this year's Prince. He feasted the assembly at his house in the parish of St. Nicolas. The house of the choristers again became the scene of the musical festivities. Seven prizes appear to have been prepared, but three only awarded, viz., the organ to Michael Fabry of Provence, a singer in the chapel of the Queen-mother; the lyre to Jehan Pennequin, master of the children of the choir of Arras cathedral; and the flute to André Tonnoys, of Mussy l'Evesque in Champagne. Nicolas de Braban, Abbé de Vallemont, Hector de Herbouville, Sieur de Briquetot, Governor and Captain of Gaillon, and Virgile Le Couvreur, a priest of Evreux Cathedral, were admitted members.

A. D. 1578.—Robert de Quenet, Abbé de Conches

---

* This composer subsequently went to Madrid at the invitation of Philip II. king of Spain. Eight masses, for five, six, and seven voices, of his composition were published at Antwerp in 1578.

et de la Noe, was this year elected Prince. He was
assisted (as the records express it,) during the whole of
the solemnity by the Duchess of Aumalle, and provided
the entertainment at his own charges at the residence
of the Bishop. The festival was, for some unexplained
reason, held at the Deanery instead of the choristers'
house. Five prizes were given ;—the organ to Esti-
enne Testart, master of the choristers of the Holy
Chapel at Paris ; the harp and the Triumph to Jehan
Planson, organist of the collegiate church of St. Germain de l'Auxerrois at Paris ; the lute to Jehan Mal-
lety ;* and the lyre to Robert Gossu, chapel-master to
Monsignor d'Aumalle at the Chateau d'Ennet. Charles
of Lorraine, Duke of Aumalle, and Nicolas Delivet,
valet-de-chambre in ordinary to the king, were admitted of the society at this festival. Du Buz, organist
of the cathedral, and one of the founders of the festival,
died in the course of this year. The names of Mauxe
and Ollivier Challumeau, two of the founders, were
erased from the list of members, they neither being
present at the festival, nor sending any excuse.

A. D. 1579.—The festival was this year holden at the
canonal residence of the treasurer of the cathedral,
whose brother, Jacques Boullenc, Sieur d'Angerville la
Riviere, was the Prince of the year. The entertainment was given, at the Prince's cost, in the same place.

---

* This composer was a native of St. Maximin in Provence.
A composition of his entitled " Les Amours de Ronsard," set
to music of four parts, was published at Paris in 1558.

Five prizes were offered, but it does not appear that any of them was awarded, neither is there anything to account for so uncommon an occurrence. Claude de Maillet, Sieur de Corneuille, was the only person this year received into the confraternity.

A. D. 1580.—This year the festival was held at the choristers' house. The entertainment was provided by Robert Feret, curé du Parc and canon of the cathedral, (the Prince of the year,) at his official residence. Of four prizes two only were adjudged;—one, the harp, to Robert Gossu, one of the successful candidates in 1578, and the other, the lyre, to Jehan Girard, a singer and chaplain in the cathedral, who was also received into the association.

A. D. 1581.—" Maistre Jehan la Biche, advocat au siege presidial," was elected Prince for this year. In point of liberality and generosity he exceeded all his predecessors. Not only did he entertain the company at dinner and supper on the feast day and at breakfast and supper on the morrow, at the Chateau of Evreux, but he also invited to the festival several of the king's chapel and chamber singers, (who sang both at the cathedral and the Chateau, where the festival was this year held,) and maintained them for seven days, and defrayed all their charges as well as those of their attendants and horses, in coming from and returning to Paris. These invited musicians were MM. Beaulieu and de Lauriny, basses; M. Salmon, tenor; M. Balifre, counter-tenor; M. Bucerat, a gentleman possessing a voice of unusual compass, as he is described as apt either for tenor, counter-tenor, or treble ; M. Mesme, a treble ; and M. Delivet, cornet to the king, one of the brethren. Four prizes were given and awarded ;—the organ to Jacques Mauduit, of Paris, Registrar of the Court of Requests in the Palace ;* the harp to Michel Nicole, of Paris ; the lute to Germain le Boudier, master of the children of the choir of Notre Dame at Nantes ; and the lyre to Michel Fabry. No new members were admitted in this or either of the next four years.

A. D. 1582.—Nicolas de Braban, Abbé de Vallemont, was appointed Prince for this year, but was prevented assisting at the festival, being detained at Gaillon by the Cardinal de Bourbon on urgent affairs. He, however, remitted thirty crowns to provide an entertain-

---

* Mauduit was born in Paris, 15th September, 1557. He received a liberal education, and in his youth travelled into Italy. He studied music with such success that he was called, even in his lifetime, "the Father of music." He is said to have been the first French musician who introduced viols in concert. His first important work was a Requiem, composed for the funeral of the poet Ronsard, afterwards performed at that of Henry IV., and subsequently at his own. His other compositions, consisting of masses, motetts, hymns, fancies and songs, were very numerous. His place in the Court of Requests was hereditary, and descended to him from his father. The preservation of the works of Claude Le Jeune is said to have been owing to Mauduit, who, when the composer was seized at the gate of St. Denis as a Huguenot, rescued his books from a soldier who was about to throw them into the flames. Mauduit died 16th August, 1627. His portrait is inserted in the *Harmonie Universelle* of Mersenne.

ment, but the brethren, with most commendable and self-denying economy, disbursed only nine crowns of that sum. Two prizes only, out of four, were allotted, viz.,—the harp to Michel Malherbe, master of the children of the choir of the cathedral of Constance ; and the lyre to Nicolas Mazouyer, who held the like appointment at the cathedral of Austun in Burgundy. The festival was held at the Canonal house of St. John Baptist, opposite the cathedral.

A. D. 1583.—In this year Thomas Du Vivier, procureur du roi at Evreux, was Prince, and the festival was held at his house called de Lyeurray, in the parish of St. Nicolas, where also the entertainment (of which he bore the charges,) was given. He obtained the assistance of the singers of the Cardinal de Guise's chapel, viz., Renè de la Grange and Gabriel Leblond, children ; Pierre Guedron, counter-tenor ; Michel Fabry, the chapel-master, (the gainer of the prize organ in 1577, and of the lyre in 1581,) tenor ; and Guillaume Briot, " a most harmonious bass." Delivet, the cornet player, one of the brethren, also attended. All these assisted both in the church and at the festival. Their travelling expences from St. Germain-en-Laye and back were borne by the Prince. Orlando de Lasso again obtained the prize organ ; Abraham Blondet, a Parisian, gained the harp ;* Eustache du Caurroy (who

---

* Blondet was a canon of the cathedral of Notre Dame at Paris. He composed in 1606 for the Royal Academy the music of a ballet entitled Ceciliade, and in 1611 published music for the church offices on St. Cecilia's day.

had received prizes in 1575 and 1576,) was awarded the lute, and Robert Gossu (who had also twice previously been a successful candidate,) obtained the lyre.

A. D. 1584.—Jehan Guiffard, one of the canons of the cathedral was this year Prince. The festival and entertainment were held at the Deanery. The Prince not only provided the entertainment at his own charges, but also maintained for five days the singers of the chapel of M. d'O. (the conductor of whom, M. Toussaint Savary, gained the prize organ for the best motett,) and the musicians of the Abbé de Vallemont, one of whom, Pascal de l'Estocart,* won the prize harp as the composer of the second best motett. Robert Gossu again obtained the prize lute, and Nicolas Morel, Master of the choristers of Rouen Cathedral, received the lyre.

A. D. 1585.—This year Claude de Maillet, Sieur de Corneuille, was elected Prince, and following the example of his predecessor, obtained the assistance at this festival of many excellent singers; amongst others, Pierre Le Large, a bass in the service of the queen-mother, and Guy Le Page, of Chartres, a domestic of the Abbé de Vallemont. The festival and entertainment were both kept at the canonal house of M. de Blanfossé,—the prince (according to what had now be-

---

* This composer published at Lyons in 1582, *Octonaires de la Vanité du monde, à trois, quatre, cinq et six voix.* Also *Les Psaumes en vers Latins et Français, mis en chant à quatre parties, distingués en plusieurs livres, en forme de motets,* and *Mélanges de chansons Latines et Françaises.*

come the custom,) defraying the charges of the latter. The prizes were distributed as follows:—the organ to Adrian Allou, Master of the choristers of St. Martin at Tours; the harp to Francis Habert, master in the church of St. Gatian at Tours; the lute to Robert Goussu, and the lyre to Pierre Quitrée, master of the choristers of la Saussaye.

A. D. 1586.—Jehan Du Pray, canon of the cathedral, was chosen Prince, and the festival was kept, and an entertainment (at his cost,) given at his official residence, St. Anne's House. The prize organ was adjudged to Robert Goussu, being the sixth prize he had obtained at these festivals, the latter four being achieved in successive years; the harp to Regolo Vecoli of Lucca;* the lute to Nicolas Morel, who had gained the lyre in 1584; and the lyre to Pierre Le Martinel of Constance in Normandy. Robert Goussu was this year admitted of the fraternity, (a distinction he had fairly earned,) as were also (at the request of their father,) Jehan, Thomas and Charles, sons of Jehan Le Biche, one of the founders. Several of the brethren had died since the last admission of members.

A. D. 1587.—Jacques Le Battelier, advocat au siége presidial, being elected Prince, provided at his own expence, as usual, an entertainment at his house opposite the chateau. Raymond de la Cassaigne, (who had ob-

---

* A set of Canzonets by this composer was published at Venice in 1569, and a set of madrigals for five voices at Lyons in 1577.

tained the prize harp in 1575,) this year gained the prize organ; Abraham Fourdy of Orleans, the harp; Denys Caignet, chapel master to M. de Villeroy,* the lute; and Pierre Le Terrier, the lyre. Nine new members were admitted, amongst them Roch d'Argillières, an organ builder, who contributed to the fund half a ducat only, but agreed to attend every St. Cecilia's day to tune the organ.

A. D. 1588.—Jehan Boette, the master of the choristers, was this year chosen Prince. The festival was kept at the Choristers' House, where the Prince entertained the brethren at a plain dinner and supper on the feast day and at breakfast on the morrow. Nicolas Vauquet, master of the choristers of the collegiate church of St. Benoist, at Paris, was the winner of the organ; the harp was obtained by Daniel Guichart, master of the choristers at Chinon; the lute by Jacques Peris of Provence, and the lyre by Toussaint Savary. Three persons were admitted brethren.

A. D. 1589.—Jehan Berthault, a priest, chaplain, and bass singer in the cathedral, was appointed Prince. He was probably a man of limited means, and therefore incapable of supporting the profuse hospitality which had distinguished so many of his predecessors, since we find that he resorted to the assistance of the brethren to provide the entertainment. He exerted himself,

---

* Caignet set to music, for four voices, a version of the Psalms of David by Philip Desportes, which was published at Paris in 1607.

however, with great and cheerful industry in the more important matter of obtaining a good performance of the music, to which end he procured the assistance of several singers; amongst others of Du Camp, a bass singer in the king's chapel. The prize organ was adjudged to Jehan Boette the younger, the harp and the lute to Jacques Péris, and the lyre to Raulin Dumont of Rouen.

A. D. 1590.—François Martin, a priest and chaplain of St. John's Chapel, and " *distributeur*" in ordinary to the chapter, was elected Prince. He entertained his brethren at dinner on the feast day and at breakfast on the morrow, receiving the like assistance as his predecessor. The " puy de musicque" was not, however, celebrated this year " because of the troubles ;" *i. e.* the internecine wars which had long disturbed France, and which then raged with increased violence by reason of the assumption of the crown by Henry IV.

A. D. 1591.—Achilles de la Presle, curé d'Eccauville, was Prince, and gave, by the assistance of the brethren, a dinner on St. Cecilia's day, but the troubles again prevented the celebration of the festival.

After this time no further mention is made in the records of the festival of either any distribution of prizes or any obstacles to the holding the festival. A Prince was elected annually until 1600, and the religious ceremonies no doubt continued to be maintained, but, from the silence of the records, it is to be presumed that no

K

secular celebration took place between 1589 and 1600. The Princes from 1591 to 1599 were as under:—

1592.—Nicolas Le Bel, singer and chaplain in the cathedral.

1593.—Noel Guillart, Sieur de Convenant, advocate in the Court of the Parliament.

1594.—Jehan Le Vavasseur, chaplain of St. Michael's Chapel in the Cathedral.

1595.—Laurens Chartier, *procureur du roi* in Evreux.

1596.—François de Langle, chaplain and organist of the cathedral.

1597.—Joseph Le Mercier, Sieur de la Ringuette, Secretary to Cardinal de Bourbon.

1598.—Michel Le Flament, formerly a choir boy in the cathedral.

1599.—Challumeau.

A. D. 1600.—The festival appears to have been resumed in this year, when Jehan Le Mercyer, canon of the cathedral, was Prince, and gave an entertainment at his own charges, after the custom of so many of his predecessors. The entertainment and festival were held at his canonal house, St. Martin's.

A. D. 1601.—Louys de la Rocque, son of the M. de la Rocque who was Prince in 1573, was this year elected Prince; and in the next year Jehan Girard, chaplain and singer in the cathedral, was chosen to perform the same duty. These persons are the last recorded as having been appointed to the office, and here, indeed, the records of the celebrations may be said to terminate, as although persons were elected members of the fraternity as late as 1612 (in which year no fewer than eleven were admitted), no reference whatever is made in the records to either ecclesiastical or secular celebrations after this time. The "Well of Music" in Evreux, which its founders no doubt fondly imagined would prove inexhaustible, seems to have gradually dried up.

The records of this institution, which had been preserved in the archives of the Chapter of Evreux, were printed in the year 1837, under the care of MM. Bonnin and Chassant, members of an Historical Record Commission, from whose publication the foregoing particulars are taken. The books in which the prize compositions were entered MM. Bonnin and Chassant were, unfortunately, unable to discover; indeed, the only information obtained by them beyond that appearing on the records was an entry in an obituary belonging to the cathedral of Evreux for the year 1774, from which it appears that in that year some extraordinary ceremonies were observed on St. Cecilia's day, and that on the morrow a mass was said for the departed brethren of the confraternity of St. Cecilia. Thus it would seem not improbable that, notwithstanding the decay and dissolution of the secular festival, the authorities of the Cathedral of Evreux continued, until, perhaps, the time of the Revolution, faithfully to perform the contract entered into by their predecessors in 1573.

Besides the matters connected with the festival at Evreux, the writer has met with but one composition having reference to the celebration of St. Cecilia's day in France, viz. an " Antienne de Ste. Cecile," for two voices (soprano and barytone), with instrumental accompaniments for viols, which is contained in the *Motets a deux Voix, avec la Basse-continue, de Mr. H. Du Mont, Abbé de Silly & Maistre de la Musique de la Chapelle du Roy*, published at Paris in 1668.

Several of the modern singing societies in Paris and other towns of France are called by the title " Cecilien," but it is not, as far as the writer is aware, the custom of any of these bodies to hold any celebration on St. Cecilia's day.

CHAPTER VII.

Continental Celebrations continued. — Italy. — Germany.—Spain.—Brazil.—Conclusion.

 FEW brief notices of the musical celebrations on St. Cecilia's day in other countries must suffice for our purpose. These might, possibly, be extended by researches in the various places in which such celebrations have been held. What is here shown will, however, be ample to prove how generally the custom of maintaining these observances has prevailed in civilized communities.

In Italy, " the land of song," and the native country of St. Cecilia, the anniversary of the Saint's martyrdom appears to have been little celebrated except as a church festival. The oratorio by Colombani before mentioned, and other similar works, were probably performed on the feast day in the churches dedicated to St. Cecilia, in the same manner as the " holy tragedies" mentioned by Riccoboni. Some masses entitled " de Saint Cecile," by Italian composers, are extant, amongst others one for sixteen voices, composed in 1646 by Paolo Petti, and another for five voices, with orchestral accompaniments, by Alessandro Scarlatti. These were, most likely, written for performance on the feast day. The late Mr. Gardiner, in his volume on Sights in Italy (1847), after speaking of his visit to the Academy of St. Cecilia at Rome, mentions having " attended the " annual performance on St. Cecilia's day in the church " dedicated to that Saint." The only secular festivity on the day in Italy which has come under notice occurred at the beginning of the eighteenth century, when Cardinal Ottoboni celebrated St. Cecilia's day by a great congress of musicians ; various compositions expressly written being performed on the occasion.

Dr. Burney, in the account of his tour through Germany in 1772, mentions a performance of Handel's music to Alexander's Feast, which had been given some time before at Florence by Lord Cowper, then British ambassador at that city. He does not, however, say on what occasion this took place. Handel's music was adapted to " a literal Italian translation given *totidem* " *syllabis*, in order to preserve the music as entire as " possible. But this tenderness for the musician (says " the Doctor,) was so much at the expence of the " poet, that Dryden's divine ode became not only " unpoetical, but unintelligible in this wretched version." A manuscript score of the music, with this Italian version, is now preserved in the library of the Sacred Harmonic Society. There is a slight alteration of the work as regards its division into parts. The air, " The " prince, unable to conceal his pain," which is placed by Handel at the end of the first part, where it is followed by a repetition of the chorus, " The many rend " the skies," is, in the Italian version, made to com-

mence the second part, doubtless for the purpose of
avoiding a second performance of the chorus. The
music of this ode, Dr. Burney informs us, was afterwards " performed at Vienna to the same words, and
" many parts of it were very much liked, in despite of
" the nonsense through which it was conveyed to the
" ears of the audience." He further says, " Gluck
" was exceedingly struck with the thoughts of our great
" poet and wished to have an ode on the same subject,
" but written on a different plan, which would preserve
" as many of them as possible. His idea was this ;
" a poem of so great a length could never be sung to
" modern music by *one person.* Now, as Dryden's
" Ode is all *narrative,* there seems no propriety in dis-
" tributing it among different persons in the perform-
" ance. He wished, therefore, to have it thrown into
" a dramatic form, in which the interlocutors might
" speak what passion suggests ; and this has been done
" in the following manner : it begins with the feast of
" Bacchus, at which Alexander and Thais preside.
" They agree to call in Timotheus to sing to them ;
" but before his arrival, the hero and his mistress differ
" in opinion concerning his merit ; the one supposes
" him to be inferior to what has been reported of him,
" and the other, superior. This contention enlivens
" the dialogue and interests the audience till the arrival
" of the bard, who begins to sing of the Trojan war,
" which animates Alexander so much, that he breaks
" out into the complaints attributed to him by the old
" story of having no Homer, like Achilles, to record

" his actions."* Dr. Burney does not inform us whether
or not this composition was intended for any observance
of St. Cecilia's day; neither does he acquaint us with
Gluck's opinion on Handel's music,—an omission much
to be lamented, since few things in musical history are
more interesting than the opinions expressed by eminent
composers of the works of their great predecessors.

In another work Dr. Burney has furnished us with
the following account of the manner of celebrating the
church service on St. Cecilia's day at Vienna about the
year 1784. " On St. Cecilia's day there is a grand
" musical performance at St. Stephen's Cathedral, the
" metropolitan church, at which, besides the performers
" on the choir establishment, all the most eminent
" foreigners, as well as natives in Vienna at the time,
" are ambitious to assist. The great mass, or choral
" music, is usually of the composition of the present
" Maestro di Capella, Hoffmann, or of Reuter, Caldara,
" or Fuchs. This performance, as well as that of the
" vespers, on the eve of St. Cecilia, is less remarkable
" for the number of hands and voices, which amount
" only to about a hundred, than for the excellence of
" the composition, and talents of the several musicians
" who exert themselves on the occasion, and who, be-

---

* A German version of Dryden's ode was made by C. W.
Ramler, and adapted to the music of Handel: it is entitled
" Alexander's Fest, oder, die Gewalt der Musik," and was
printed at Leipsic with the score of the music which included
the accompaniments added by Mozart. A cantata entitled
" Timoteo, oder, Die Macht der Töne," taken from Dryden's
poem and set by Winter, was published at Leipsic in 1809.

" tween the different parts of the service, perform con-
" certos, with solo parts, to display their powers on their
" several instruments."

The yearly custom of musicians celebrating St. Cecilia's day prevailed in Germany as early as the sixteenth century. It is alluded to in a curious Latin
poem entitled *Convivium Cantorum*, written by Ger-
hard de Roo, a Netherlander, and published at Munich
in 1585, every word of which commences with the
letter C.

An allusion to some musical celebration on St. Cecilia's day in the Spanish metropolis occurs in Thomas
Killegrew's play, " Thomaso, or the Wanderer." This
piece was published in 1664, but was written some
years before, during Killegrew's residence in Madrid,
where the scene is laid. One of the characters, Seru-
lina, says: " 'Tis now St. Cecilia's Eve, his own feast,
" get our veils, and let us go in disguise to the Cale-
" travos ; *There's the great Musick to-morrow*, and we
" shall certainly meet him at the Vespers. He was
" always a devotee to the fair Cecilia and Doña Fran-
" cisca ; Musick was ever his delight, but their voices
" especially."

It appears from a communication made by M. Neu-
komm to the *Allgemeine Musikalische Zeitung* in 1820,
that St. Cecilia's day was then annually celebrated at
Rio de Janeiro by the Corporation of Resident Musicians, called in Portuguese, Irmandade. This Corporation (which was a sort of religious association,) also
had a Requiem for departed musicians performed a few
days after the feast-day. In December, 1819, a por-

tion of the Office for the Dead, set to music by David
Perez, and Mozart's Requiem were performed on this
occasion in the Church of do Parto by a powerful
orchestra under the direction of Jozè Mauricio Nunes
Garcia, the royal chapel-master. This was the first
time of the master-work of Mozart being heard in the
New World.

The most modern composition on the subject of St.
Cecilia's day is an ode, or cantata, set by J. B. Van
Bree of Amsterdam in 1845 ; but this was not produced to celebrate the Saint's festival, but the birthday
of a Dutch princess. An English version was performed
in 1846 by the Choral Harmonists, an amateur association whose meetings were held at the London Tavern.

Some of the German singing societies, particularly
those in the Rhenish provinces, are, as the writer is
informed, accustomed to keep St. Cecilia's day as a kind
of musical holiday, but no especial reference to the
occasion is introduced into their performances.

It is unnecessary to enter upon a consideration of the
questions which seem naturally to arise out of the subject of this work, as to whether or not a revival of
the custom of celebrating an annual festival in praise
of music, accompanied or not by the award of prizes
for the most excellent compositions and poems having
reference to the occasion, would be beneficial to the
musical art ;—or whether or not the continuance of
that portion of the ceremonial which included attendance at Divine service would have the effect of ensuring
a constant supply of new compositions for our noble

choral service, and so rendering the festival auxiliary to one of the highest of purposes, a provision for the worthy maintenance of the public worship of Almighty God.

Impressed with a strong feeling that the former celebrations must have contributed in no small degree to promote the culture and practice of music, both sacred and secular, in England, the writer has, in the preceding pages, attempted, however feebly, to supply the omission of our musical historians, and furnish some account of the Musical celebrations on St. Cecilia's day.

APPENDIX.

A COLLECTION OF ODES ON

ST. CECILIA'S DAY.

APPENDIX.

ODE FOR ST. CECILIA'S DAY, 1683,

BY CHRISTOPHER FISHBURN.

Set to Music by Henry Purcell.

WELCOME to all the pleasures that delight
Of ev'ry sense the grateful appetite !
Hail, great assembly of Apollo's race !
Hail to this happy place,
This Musical assembly, that seems to be
The ark of universal harmony !

Here the deities approve
(The God of Music and of Love,)
All the talents they have lent you,
All the blessings they have sent you ;
Pleas'd to see what they bestow
Live and thrive so well below ;
While joys celestial their bright souls invade,
To find what great improvement you have made.
Then lift up your voices, those organs of nature,
Those charms to the troubled and amorous creature :
The Power shall divert us a pleasanter way ;

For Sorrow and Grief
Find from Music relief,
And Love its soft charms must obey.

Beauty, thou source of love,
And Virtue, thou innocent fire,
Made by the Powers above
To temper the heat of desire ;
Music, that fancy employs
In raptures of innocent flame,
We offer with lute and with voice
To Cecilia, Cecilia's bright name :
In a concert of voices, while instruments play,
With Music we'll celebrate this holiday ;
In a concert of voices we'll sing, Iô Cecilia !

ODE FOR ST. CECILIA'S DAY, 1683,

Author unknown.   Composed by Henry Purcell.

R AISE, raise the voice, all instruments obey,
   Let the sweet lute its softest notes display,
For this is sacred Music's holiday.
The God himself says, he'll be present here,
Dress'd in his brightest beams he will appear,
Not to the eye, but to the ravish'd ear.

Hark ! I hear Apollo cry,
" Crown the day with harmony !
" And let ev'ry gen'rous heart
" In the chorus bear a part."

Mark, mark, how readily each pliant string
Prepares itself, and as an offering,
The tribute of some gentle sound does bring.
Then altogether in harmonious lays,
To the sublimest pitch themselves they raise,
And loudly celebrate their Master's praise.

Come, raise up your voices, and let us dispute
For melodious notes with the viol and lute :
Apollo's delighted with what we have done,
And, clapping his hands, cries, " Iô, go on ;"
With a smile, he does all our endeavours approve,
And vows he ne'er heard such a concert above.

ODE

" FOR AN ANNIVERSARY OF MUSICK KEPT UPON ST. CECILIA'S DAY," 1684.

BY JOHN OLDHAM.

Set to Music by Dr. John Blow.

BEGIN the song ! your instruments advance !
        Tune the voice and tune the flute,
        Touch the silent, sleeping lute,
And make the strings to their own measures dance.
Bring gentlest thought that into language glide,
Bring softest words that into numbers slide :
        Let ev'ry heart, let ev'ry tongue,
        To make the noble concert throng :
Let all in one harmonious note agree
        To frame the mighty song,
For this is Music's sacred jubilee.

L

Hark ! how the waken'd strings resound,
And sweetly break the yielding air !
The ravish'd sense how pleasingly they wound,
And call the list'ning soul into the ear !
Each pulse beats time, and ev'ry heart
With tongue and fingers bears a part.
    By harmony's entrancing pow'r
When we are thus wound up to extacy,
    Methinks we mount, methinks we tow'r,
And seem to antedate our future bliss on high.

How dull were life, how hardly worth our care,
    But for the charms which Music lends !
    How pall'd its pleasures would appear
But for the pleasure which our art attends !
    Without the sweets of melody
    To tune our vital breath,
    Who would not give it up to death,
And in the silent grave contented lie ?

Music's the cordial of a troubled breast,
The softest remedy that grief can find ;
The greatest spell that charms our care to rest,
And calms the ruffled passions of the mind.
    Music does all our joys refine,
    It gives the relish to our wine,
    'Tis that gives rapture to our love,
And wings devotion to a pitch divine ;
'Tis our chief bliss on earth, and half our heav'n above.

Come then with tuneful breath and string,

The praises of our art let's sing;
 Let's sing to blest Cecilia's fame,
That grac'd this art, and gave this day its name;
 With music, wine, and mirth conspire
To bear a concert, and make up the quire!

ODE FOR ST. CECILIA'S DAY, 1685.

BY NAHUM TATE.

Set to Music by William Turner.

TUNE the viol, touch the lute,
 Wake the harp, inspire the flute,
Call the jolly swains away;
Love and Music reign to day.

Let your kids and lambkins rove,
 Let them sport or feed at will,
 Grace the vale, or climb the hill;
Let them feed, or let them love,
Let them love, or let them stray,
Let them feed, or let them play;
 Neglect them or guide them,
 No harm shall betide them,
On bright Cecilia's, bright Cecilia's day.

 Thus the nymphs and jolly swains
 Kindly mingled on the plains,
 In delightful measure move,
 Full of joy, and full of love;

With their cheerful roundelay
Celebrate Cecilia's day,
While Angels join in concert from above.

What charms can Music not impart,
That through the ear finds passage to the heart !
In vain the Muse indites a lover's tale,
 In vain his doleful words declare
 His passion to the cruel fair ;
'Tis Music only makes his song prevail.
This only can her scorn controul ;
 In vain do wit and sense combine,
 Without this art to make our numbers shine :
Words are the body, Music is the soul.

 Call the jolly swains away,
 To celebrate Cecilia's day.
 Rouse the viol, wake the lyre,
To sing her praise who did our art inspire :
 Let victorious heroes stay,—
  At leisure we will do them right ;
 To our own art we consecrate this day,
  And Music best can Music's power recite.

" ON THE FEAST OF CECILIA, 1686,
AN ODE."

BY THOMAS FLETCHER.

IO ! with triumphant noise,
   With Music's loudest voice
This day a solemn feast proclaim,
A solemn feast to great Cecilia's name.
  No cloudy thought, no sullen tear,
  No tumultuous care or fear
Approach the limits of this sacred day,
Sacred to Music and Cecilia ;
  But all be sweet, serene, and gay ;
Sweet as the Saint to whom these rites we pay ;
Sweet as the notes she did below, or now above does
    play.

  Music, thou only perfect joy,
   Which neither present fears allay,
    Nor after pangs destroy !
The dear remembrance of the pleasure past
    Shall no repentance cost,
    Bring with it no regret,
   But be, like its own echo, sweet.
Music, thou mighty soul o' th' Universe !
   Which dost, like (thine own god,) the sun,
   Thro' all thine active pow'r disperse,
And all the stupid mass with life and beauty crown :
Methinks I now behold sweet Orpheus sit

On Strymon's bank, and tune his lyre
To sounds which life and vig'rous joys inspire:
Round him the list'ning beasts their food forget,
       Forget to play,
And without motion round the charmer stay.
But nimbler trees, when they the music hear,
   (Music which gives them ear,)
  Leap forth, and wanton round the place;
Trees skip, like beasts; beasts stand unmov'd, like trees.
Pines, elms, and cedars in long rows advance,
   An aged oak leads up the dance:
Two hundred years it stood the wood's chief pride,
So long Jove's bolts and struggling winds defied;
Now from its bed of earth away it tears,
And round its spreading roots a weighty mountain bears.

  Hark! hark! th' harmonious accents move,
Thro' the brisk air th' enliven'd numbers rove;
   About they dance, about they play,
   And call the ravish'd soul away:
The soul th' harmonious summons does obey;
The soul which is itself all harmony.
With all its sprightly trains of faculties,
   Out at the ear it flies.
Hence 'tis, that oft with height of extacy
   We faint and die away.
  The soul, in haste to be at large,
   And heedless of its charge,
Leaves almost uninform'd the stupid clay.
  Now o'er the trembling strings it bounds,
Now thro' the air pursues the flitting sounds;

Then lured back again
  By some more gentle strain,
  Calm and languishing it lies,
Grasping the newborn accents as they rise;
Greets all th' harmonious brethren as they pass;
  Does each soft note embrace:
  And fain would here acquainted grow
    With that, that only joy
  Which of all those we seem to have below
Shall with itself share immortality.

To thee, Cecilia, guardian Saint, to thee
This tribute of our time and art we pay.
While thou in lofty thoughts and sweetest lays
  Exalt'st thy Maker's praise,
We (tho' in humbler verse, in coarser strain,)
  Presume to prattle thine.
Music, dear Saint, is both thy bliss and care,
Above thou enjoy'st it, and protect'st it here,
  So that 'tis hard to say,
Thou blessest Music most, or Music thee.

Then sooner let the rolling year forget,
  Among its num'rous train,
  To bring this happy day again,
Than we its yearly rites to celebrate:
And let each sweet intelligence above,
  Which to harmonious sounds does move
    His golden sphere,
  When he beholds the glitt'ring day
Return, and in the dance of time appear,
Strike the chords full, and make an universal symphony.

" A SONG FOR ST. CECILIA'S DAY, 1687,"

BY JOHN DRYDEN.

Originally composed by Giovanni Baptista Draghi ;
afterwards by George Frederic Handel.

FROM Harmony, from heavenly Harmony,
    This universal frame began.
When Nature underneath a heap
    Of jarring atoms lay,
    And could not heave her head,
The tuneful voice was heard from high,
    Arise, ye more than dead.
Then cold, and hot, and moist, and dry,
In order to their stations leap,
    And Music's power obey.
From Harmony, from heavenly Harmony,
    This universal frame began :
    From harmony to harmony
Through all the compass of the notes it ran,
The diapason closing full in Man.

What passion cannot Music raise and quell !
    When Jubal struck the chorded shell,
    His list'ning brethren stood around,
    And, wond'ring, on their faces fell,
    To worship that celestial sound ;
Less than a God they thought there could not dwell
    Within the hollow of that shell
    That spoke so sweetly and so well.
What passion cannot Music raise and quell !

The trumpet's loud clangour
   Excites us to arms,
With shrill notes of anger,
   And mortal alarms ;
The double, double, double beat
   Of the thund'ring drum
Cries, Hark ! the foes come ;
Charge, charge, 'tis too late to retreat.

The soft, complaining flute
In dying notes discovers
The woes of hopeless lovers,
Whose dirge is whisper'd by the warbling lute.
   Sharp violins proclaim
Their jealous pangs and desperation,
Fury, frantic indignation,
Depth of pains, and heighth of passion
   For the fair disdainful dame.

But oh ! what art can teach,
What human voice can reach
   The sacred organ's praise ?
Notes inspiring holy love,
Notes that wing their heavenly ways
   To join the choirs above.

Orpheus could lead the savage race ;
And trees uprooted left their place,
   Sequacious of the lyre.
But bright Cecilia rais'd the wonder high'r ;
When to her organ vocal breath was given,

An Angel heard, and straight appear'd,
   Mistaking earth for heaven.

As from the power of sacred lays
   The spheres began to move,
And sung the great Creator's praise
   To all the bless'd above ;
So when the last and dreadful hour
This crumbling pageant shall devour,
The trumpet shall be heard on high ;
The dead shall live, the living die,
And Music shall untune the sky.

A SONG FOR ST. CECILIA'S DAY, 1690,

BY THOMAS SHADWELL.

Set to Music by Robert King.

O SACRED Harmony, prepare our lays ;
   While on Cecilia's day we sing your praise,
From earth to heav'n our warbling voices raise.

Join all your glorious instruments around,
The yielding air with your vibrations wound,
And fill heav'ns conclave with the mighty sound.

You did at first the warring atoms join,
Made qualities most opposite combine,
While discords did with pleasing concords join.

The universe you fram'd, you still sustain ;

Without you what in tune does now remain
Would jangle into chaos once again.

It does your most transcendant glory prove,
That to complete immortal joys above,
There must be harmony to crown their love.

  Dirges with sorrow still inspire
  The doleful and lamenting quire,
  With swelling hearts and flowing eyes
  They solemnize their obsequies;
  For grief they frequent discords choose,
  Long bindings and chromatics use;
  Organs and viols sadly groan
  To the voice's dismal tone.

 If love's gentle passions we
 Express, there must be harmony:
 We touch the soft and tender flute,
 The sprinkling and melodious lute,
  When we describe the tickling smart
  Which does invade a lovesick heart:
  Sweet nymphs in pretty murmurs plain,
  All chill and panting with the pleasing pain
  Which can be eas'd by nothing but the swain.

 If poets in a lofty epic strain
 Some ancient noble history recite,
 How heroes love and puissant conquerors fight,
 Or how on cruel fortune they complain:
 Or if a Muse the fate of empires sings,

The change of crowns, the rise and fall of kings:
  'Tis sacred Music does impart
  Life and vigour to the art;
It makes the dumb poetic pictures breath,
Victors' and poets' names it saves from death.

How does the thund'ring martial song
Provoke the military throng!
The hautboys and the warlike fife,
With clamours of the deaf'ning drum,
Make peasants bravely hazard life,
And quicken those whom fears benumb!
The clangour of the trumpet's sound
Fills all the dusty place around,
And does from neighb'ring hills rebound:
Iô triumphe when we sing,
We make the trembling vallies ring.

All instruments and voices fit the quire,
While we enchanting harmony admire.
What mighty wonders by our art are taught,
What miracles by sacred numbers wrought
On earth: in heav'n no joys are perfect found
Till by celestial harmony they're crown'd.

AN ODE ON ST. CECILIA'S DAY,

BY SAMUEL WESLEY.

Set to Music by Samuel Wesley, the Author's Grandson.

BEGIN, begin the noble song,
  Call ev'ry tuneful soul into the ear,
And sweetly chain them there
  With numbers soft and strong:
Numbers, Cecilia, soft as those
Which did thy heav'nly hymns compose.
Thy beauty made the world adore,
Thy music and devotion more;
  For these our annual tribute thus we pay,
And thus, fair Saint, we hail thy bright, thy happy day.

Music and thee, fair Saint, our songs divide,
Music is ours, and thou art Music's pride.
  Its charms the whole creation sway,
  Music commands, and all obey.
Hark! hark! Arion sweeps the sounding string;
  The dolphins round him play,
  And waves that crowd his way;
  The nymphs their treasures bring;
  The Tritons' silver shells
  His softer lyre excels;
  Enchanting Syren's charms
  And Neptune's rage disarms.

How various, Music, is thy praise !
What passions canst thou calm, what courage canst thou
      raise !
   With what a natural art inspire
 Love's gentle flame, Devotion's purer fire !
To arms, to arms ! that noble, dreadful sound,
How soon it wakes our echoing souls within !
See all the hills with glitt'ring squadrons crown'd !
   See all the trembling vales around !
Cannons the warlike concert first begin,
   The trumpet's clangour rends the sky,
   The martial sounds are heard on high.

   When, heav'n-born Peace, wilt thou descend
     And tune the world again ?
   Fair Peace, the Muses' guard and friend,
     Where thou art not we sing in vain :
  You're near allied, or Music's self must be ;
  Peace, Beauty, Virtue, all are Harmony.
    For Peace the sullen warrior toils,
    The best of all his dear bought spoils ;
    For Peace the tender virgins pray,
    Strict siege around the altars make ;
    Repuls'd will no denial take,
      But sigh at heav'n's delay.

   'Tis here a sacred vestal Music turns,
    Contemns, forgets the world below,
    And while in hallow'd fire she burns,
    Does like its flames still upward go.
   This did Cecilia's happy hours employ,

Her's and her rival Angels' joy.
Cecilia's voice and organ join,
The blest look down, and think her more divine;
Again she plays, again she sings,
Applauding Angels clap their wings,
Their softest Hallelujahs try,
But cannot mend her harmony.

Iô triumph! sing and play,
'Tis Cecilia's happy day;
Louder still and still more loud,
'Till the list'ning Angels crowd,
Think 'tis their Cecilia's strain,
Think she's gone to earth again.

AN ODE

FOR THE ANNIVERSARY FEAST OF ST. CECILIA, 1691.

BY THOMAS D'URFEY.

Set to Music by Dr. John Blow.

THE glorious day is come, that will for ever be
Renown'd as Music's greatest Jubilee:
The spheres, those instruments divine,
Tun'd to Apollo's charming lyre,
The sons of all the learned Nine
With soft harmonious souls inspire;
Behold, around Parnassus' top they sit,
And heav'nly Music now vies with immortal Wit.

Couch'd by the pleasant Heliconian spring,
Of bright Cecilia they sing;
Admir'd Cecilia that informs their brains;
The awful goddess that their cause maintains;
   And with her sacred pow'r supplies
   The artful hand and tuneful voice,
And gives a taste of heav'nly bliss in more than mortal
       strains.

   And first the trumpet's part
   Inflames the hero's heart;
   The martial noise completes his joys
   And soul inspires by art:
And now he thinks he's in the field,
And now he makes the foe to yield;
Now victory does eagerly pursue,
And Music's warlike notes make ev'ry fancy true.

The battle done, all loud alarms do cease,
Hark, how the charming flutes conclude the peace;
Whose soft'ning notes make fiercest rage obey:
If Pan, beneath the famous myrtle's shade,
   To Midas half so well had play'd,
The Delphian God himself had lost the day.
Excesses of pleasure now crowd on apace;
How sweetly the violins sound to each bass,
The ravishing trebles delight ev'ry ear,
And mirth in a scene of true joy does appear:
   No lover of Phillis's rigour complains,
None mourn for their losses, or laugh for their gains;
But lost in an extacy publish their joy,

Whilst the name of Cecilia resounds to the sky.
   Ah heav'n! what is't I hear,
The warbling lute enchants mine ear:
Now beauty's pow'r inflames my breast again,
I sigh and languish with a pleasing pain.
    The notes so soft, so sweet the air,
    The soul of love must sure be there,
That mine in rapture charms, and drives away despair.

Music! celestial Music! what can be,
   On this side heav'n, compar'd to thee?
   Thou only treat fit for a deity:
Monarchs by flattery or fame
   May arrogate a glorious name,
But in each soul-delighting symphony,
   Address'd to bright Cecilia's royalty,
Are sacred honours fit for none, but for Divine degree.

This that blest king and God-like prophet knew
   That oft from worldly joys withdrew;
From glittering pomp and all the courtly throng;
   And to the Eternal King of kings,
   To the sweet harp's well-govern'd strings,
Paid best devotion in seraphic song.

      And thus by Music's pow'r
      Above dull earth we soar;
      Exalt our chorus to the sky,
      And in transporting melody,
        Cecilia's name adore.
    Divine Cecilia, whom we all confess
    Our art's inspirer; Music's patroness.

M

ODE ON ST. CECILIA'S DAY, 1692,

BY NICHOLAS BRADY.

Set to Music by Henry Purcell.

H AIL! bright Cecilia, hail! fill ev'ry heart
    With love of thee and thy celestial art;
That thine and Music's sacred love
May make the British forest prove
As famous as Dodona's vocal grove.
Hark! hark! each tree its silence breaks,
    The box and fir to talk begin!
    This in the sprightly violin,
That in the flute distinctly speaks!
'Twas sympathy their list'ning brethren drew,
When to the Thracian lyre with leafy wings they flew.

'Tis Nature's voice: by all the moving wood
        Of creatures understood:
    The universal tongue to none
    Of all her num'rous race unknown!
    From her it learn'd the mighty art
    To court the ear and strike the heart:
At once the passions to express and move;
We hear, and straight we grieve or hate, rejoice or love:
    In unseen chains it does the fancy bind;
At once it charms the sense and captivates the mind.

        Soul of the world! inspir'd by thee
        The jarring seeds of matter did agree,

Thou didst the scatter'd atoms bind,
  Which, by thy laws of true proportion join'd,
Made up of various parts one perfect harmony.
  Thou tun'dst this world below, the spheres above,
Which in the heav'nly round to their own music move.

  With that sublime celestial lay
  Dare any earthly sounds compare?
  If any earthly music dare,
      The noble organ may.
  From heav'n its wond'rous notes were giv'n,
  (Cecilia oft convers'd with heav'n,)
  Some Angel of the sacred choir
  Did with his breath the pipes inspire;
And of their notes above the just resemblance gave,
  Brisk without lightness, without dulness grave.

      Wond'rous machine!
  To thee the warbling lute,
  Though us'd to conquest, must be forc'd to yield:
  With thee unable to dispute,
      The airy violin
  And lofty viol quit the field;
  In vain they tune their speaking strings
To court the cruel fair, or praise victorious kings.
  Whilst all thy consecrated lays
  Are to more noble uses bent,
And ev'ry grateful note to heav'n repays
      The melody it lent.

In vain the am'rous flute and soft guitar

Jointly labour to inspire
Wanton heat and loose desire ;
Whilst thy chaste airs do gently move
Seraphic flames and heavenly love.
The fife and all the harmony of war
In vain attempt the passions to alarm
Which thy commanding sounds compose and charm.
Let these among themselves contest
Which can discharge its single duty best :
Thou summ'st their diff'ring graces up in one,
And art a concert of them all within thyself alone.

Hail ! bright Cecilia, hail to thee !
Great patroness of us and Harmony !
Who, whilst among the choir above
Thou dost thy former skill improve,
With rapture of delight dost see
Thy fav'rite art
Make up a part
Of infinite felicity.
Hail ! bright Cecilia, hail to thee !
Great patroness of us and Harmony !

A SONG FOR ST. CECILIA'S DAY
AT OXFORD.

BY JOSEPH ADDISON.

CECILIA, whose exalted hymns
With joy and wonder fill the blest,
In choirs of warbling seraphims
Known and distinguish'd from the rest,

Attend, harmonious Saint, and see
Thy vocal sons of harmony ;
Attend, harmonious Saint, and hear our pray'rs ;
Enliven all our earthly airs,
And, as thou sing'st thy God, teach us to sing of thee :
Tune ev'ry string and ev'ry tongue,
Be thou the muse and subject of our song.

Let all Cecilia's praise proclaim,
Employ the echo in her name.
Hark how the flutes and trumpets raise,
At bright Cecilia's name, their lays,
The organ labours in her praise.
Cecilia's name does all our numbers grace,
From ev'ry voice the tuneful accents fly,
In soaring trebles now it rises high,
And now it sinks, and dwells upon the base.
Cecilia's name through all the notes we sing,
The work of ev'ry skilful tongue,
The sound of ev'ry trembling string,
The sound and triumph of our song.

For ever consecrate the day
To music and Cecilia ;
Music, the greatest good that mortals know,
And all of heav'n we have below.
Music can noble hints impart,
Engender fury, kindle love ;
With unsuspected eloquence can move,
And manage all the man with secret art.
When Orpheus strikes the trembling lyre,

The streams stand still, the stones admire ;
The list'ning savages advance,
   The wolf and lamb around him trip,
   The bears in awkward measures leap,
  And tigers mingle in the dance.
The moving woods attended as he play'd,
And Rhodope was left without a shade.

  Music religious heat inspires,
   It wakes the soul and lifts it high,
  And wings it with sublime desires,
  And fits it to bespeak the Deity.
Th' Almighty listens to a tuneful tongue,
And seems well pleas'd and courted with a song.
  Soft moving sounds and heav'nly airs
Give force to ev'ry word and recommend our pray'rs.
  When time itself shall be no more,
  And all things in confusion hurl'd,
  Music shall then exert its pow'r,
And sound survive the ruins of the world :
  Then Saints and Angels shall agree
  In one eternal jubilee :
All heav'n shall echo with their hymns divine,
  And God Himself with pleasure see
The whole creation in a chorus join.

  Consecrate the place and day
  To Music and Cecilia.
Let no rough winds approach, nor dare
  Invade the hallow'd bounds,
Nor rudely shake the tuneful air,

Nor spoil the fleeting sounds.
Nor mournful sigh nor groan be heard,
　　But gladness dwell on ev'ry tongue ;
Whilst all, with voice and string prepar'd
　　Keep up the loud harmonious song,
And imitate the blest above
In joy, and harmony, and love.

ODE FOR ST. CECILIA'S DAY, 1693,

BY THEOPHILUS PARSONS.

Set to Music by Godfrey Finger.

CECILIA, look, look down and see
　　　A tribute paid to Harmony,
A tribute paid to heav'n and thee :
And while we Music's praise rehearse
In lower notes and fainter verse,
Warm you, great Saint, your willing choir
　　With your own celestial fire.
　　May you move on ev'ry string,
　　Warble sweets in ev'ry voice,
In ev'ry note your grateful influence sing,
And by your aid confirm our happy choice.

Eldest of arts, and universal spring
　　　Of every thing !
When beings in a dark confusion lay
　　Thy voice the sullen gloom did chase,
　　　Matter did its form embrace,

And Chaos fled before the new-born day.
　Heav'n look'd, and all things good did see,
　For each and all arose from Harmony.

Parent of all! thou still dost sway,
And o'er this lower world preside;
　Man and his passions thee obey,
As meaner waters the commanding tide,
Or that, the moon's imperious ray.
　Beauty may wound th' unguarded eyes,
And slowly creep into the heart:
　But Music quick as lightning flies;
The pleasure dances with the smart,
And melts and trills through ev'ry part.
Without the magic of the fair,
　We love, we sigh, and we despair,
We catch at sounds, and grasp the fleeting air.

Hark! hark! the trumpet calls to arm;
What vein so drowsy feels not the alarm,
And wakes not at th' inspiring charm?
　The warlike horse already paws,
　And neighs aloud his warm applause.
In vain is now the soft'ning flute,
In vain the warbling of the lute,
　Or the gay violin's persuading airs:
　The philtre glides successless through our ears,
　Ev'n Celia's voice no more can tame
　The forward hero's lust of fame;
　A charm might vanquish, if applied,
A madman's frenzy, or a woman's pride:

Temper with hope the lover's fears,
    (An April-shine to gild his tears,)
The weather of our happiness abate,
Softer than love, yet absolute as fate.

    But oh! more subtle virtue flows
    Such jarring passions to compose.
Still, still the work, O sacred Harmony, is thine:
    We hear, and straight the ruffled soul
    Is still; the billows cease to roll,
        The swelling streams decline,
    And ev'ry wounded faculty is whole.
    Thus, at the shepherd's tuneful cry,
        Divided flocks together fly:
    The rivulets their murmurs cease;
    Without a breath of wind the trees,
And smiling nature's all around at peace.

    Tune all your instruments aloud,
Glad voices mingling with the cheerful crowd;
        Sacred be your tuneful lays,
        Sacred to Cecilia's praise.
Thus we'll grateful offerings bring,
        Yearly thus her praises sing:
Till, joined in chorus with our Saint above,
        We take a nobler theme, to prove
By endless Harmony, immortal Love.

AN ODE FOR ST. CECILIA'S DAY, 1693,

BY THOMAS YALDEN.

Set to Music by Daniel Purcell.

B EGIN, and strike th' harmonious lyre !
    Let the loud instruments prepare
  To raise our souls and charm the ear,
With joys that only Music can inspire ;
  Hark how the willing strings obey !
  To consecrate this happy day
Sacred to Music, Love, and blest Cecilia.
  In lofty numbers, tuneful lays,
  We'll celebrate the Virgin's praise :
Her skilful hand first taught our strings to move,
  To her this sacred art we owe,
  Who first anticipated heav'n below,
And play'd the hymns on earth that now she sings above.

What moving charms each tuneful voice contains,
  Charms that thro' the willing ear,
  A tide of pleasing raptures bear,
And, with diffusive joys, run thrilling thro' our veins.
  The list'ning soul does sympathize,
  And with each varied note complies :
  While gay and sprightly airs delight,
  Then free from cares and unconfin'd,
It takes in pleasing extacies its flight.
  With mournful sounds a sadder garb it wears,
  Indulges grief and gives a loose to tears.

Music's the language of the blest above,
 No voice but Music's can express
 The joys that happy souls possess,
Nor in just raptures tell the wond'rous pow'r of love.
 'Tis nature's dialect, design'd
 To charm and to instruct the mind.
  Music's an universal good!
 That does dispense its joys around,
 In all the elegance of sound,
To be by men admir'd, by Angels understood.

Let ev'ry restless passion cease to move!
  And each tumultuous thought obey
  The happy influence of this day,
  For Music's unity and love.
Music's the soft indulger of the mind,
  The kind diverter of our care,
The surest refuge mournful grief can find;
A cordial to the breast and charm to ev'ry ear.
 Thus when the Prophet struck his tuneful lyre,
  Saul's evil genius did retire:
  In vain were remedies applied,
  In vain all other arts were tried;
His hand and voice alone the charm could find
To heal his body and compose his mind.

Now let the trumpet's louder voice proclaim
   A solemn jubilee:
  For ever sacred let it be,
To skilful Jubal's, and Cecilia's name.
  Great Jubal, author of our lays,

Who first the hidden charms of Music found ;
    And thro' their airy paths did trace
    The secret springs of sound.
    When from his hollow chorded shell
    The soft melodious accents fell,
    With wonder and delight he play'd,
While the harmonious strings his skilful hand obey'd.

But fair Cecilia to a pitch divine
    Improv'd her artful lays ;
When to the organ she her voice did join,
    In the Almighty's praise ;
Then choirs of list'ning Angels stood around,
Admir'd her art, and blest the heav'nly sound.
    Her praise alone no tongue can reach,
    But in the strains herself can teach :
    Then let the voice and lyre combine,
    And in a tuneful concert join ;
    For Music's her reward and care,
Above she enjoys it, and protects it here.

    Then kindly treat this happy day,
    And grateful honours to Cecilia pay :
    To her these lov'd harmonious rites belong,
To her that tunes our strings and still inspires our song.

ODE,

Author unknown.   Composed prior to 1700,

By Dr. John Blow.

WELCOME, welcome, ev'ry guest,
　　Welcome to the Muses' feast!
Music is your only cheer,
Music entertains the ear.
The sacred Nine observe the mode,
And bring you dainties from abroad;
The delicious Thracian lute
And Dodona's mellow flute,
With Cremona's racy fruit.
At home you have the freshest air,
Vocal, instrumental fare;
Our English trumpet nothing has surpast:
The Carnival has not so rich a taste.

ALEXANDER'S FEAST, OR THE POWER OF MUSIC.

AN ODE IN HONOUR OF ST. CECILIA'S DAY, 1697.

BY JOHN DRYDEN:

*Originally composed by Jeremiah Clark; afterwards
by George Frederic Handel.*

'TWAS at the royal feast, for Persia won,
　　By Philip's warlike son:
　　Aloft in awful state

The godlike hero sate
On his imperial throne :
His valiant peers were plac'd around ;
Their brows with roses and with myrtles bound :
(So should desert in arms be crown'd.)
The lovely Thais, by his side,
Sate like a blooming Eastern bride,
In flower of youth and beauty's pride.
Happy, happy, happy pair !
None but the brave,
None but the brave,
None but the brave deserves the fair.

Timotheus, plac'd on high,
Amid the tuneful quire,
With flying fingers touch'd the lyre :
The trembling notes ascend the sky,
And heav'nly joys inspire.
The song began from Jove,
Who left his blissful seats above,
(Such is the power of mighty love)
A dragon's fiery form belied the god :
Sublime on radiant spires he rode,
When he to fair Olympia prest ;
And while he sought her snowy breast :
Then, round her slender waist he curl'd,
And stamp'd an image of himself, a sov'reign of the world.
The list'ning crowd admire the lofty sound,
A present deity, they shout around :
A present deity, the vaulted roofs rebound :
With ravish'd ears

The monarch hears,
Assumes the god,
Affects to nod,
And seems to shake the spheres.

The praise of Bacchus then the sweet musician sung;
Of Bacchus, ever fair and ever young;
The jolly god in triumph comes;
Sound the trumpets; beat the drums;
Flush'd with a purple grace,
He shows his honest face:
Now give the hautboys breath; he comes, he comes.
Bacchus, ever fair and young,
Drinking joys did first ordain;
Bacchus' blessings are a treasure,
Drinking is the soldier's pleasure;
Rich the treasure,
Sweet the pleasure;
Sweet is pleasure after pain.

Sooth'd with the sound, the king grew vain;
Fought all his battles o'er again;
And thrice he routed all his foes; and thrice he slew
the slain.
The master saw the madness rise;
His glowing cheeks, his ardent eyes;
And, while he heaven and earth defied,
Chang'd his hand, and check'd his pride.
He chose a mournful muse
Soft pity to infuse:
He sung Darius great and good,

By too severe a fate,
Fallen, fallen, fallen, fallen,
Fallen from his high estate,
   And welt'ring in his blood.
Deserted, at his utmost need,
By those his former bounty fed:
On the bare earth expos'd he lies,
With not a friend to close his eyes.
With downcast looks the joyless victor sate,
  Revolving in his alter'd soul
    The various turns of chance below;
  And, now and then, a sigh he stole,
    And tears began to flow.

The mighty master smil'd to see
That love was in the next degree:
'Twas but a kindred sound to move,
For pity melts the mind to love.
  Softly sweet, in Lydian measures,
  Soon he sooth'd his soul to pleasures.
War, he sung, is toil and trouble;
Honour but an empty bubble;
  Never ending, still beginning,
Fighting still and still destroying,
  If the world be worth thy winning,
Think, O think it worth enjoying:
  Lovely Thais sits beside thee,
  Take the good the gods provide thee.
The many rend the skies with loud applause;
So Love was crown'd, but Music won the cause.
  The prince, unable to conceal his pain,

    Gaz'd on the fair
    Who caus'd his care,
  And sigh'd and look'd, sigh'd and look'd,
  Sigh'd and look'd, and sigh'd again:
At length, with love and wine at once opprest,
The vanquish'd victor sunk upon her breast.

Now strike the golden lyre again:
A louder yet, and yet a louder strain.
Break his bands of sleep asunder,
And rouse him, like a rattling peal of thunder.
  Hark, hark, the horrid sound
    Has rais'd up his head:
    As awak'd from the dead,
  And amaz'd, he stares around.
Revenge, revenge, Timotheus cries,
  See the Furies arise:
    See the snakes that they rear
    How they hiss in their hair,
And the sparkles that flash from their eyes!
  Behold, a ghastly band,
  Each a torch in his hand!
Those are Grecian ghosts, that in battle were slain,
      And unburied remain
     Inglorious on the plain:
    Give the vengeance due
    To the valiant crew.
Behold how they toss their torches on high,
  How they point to the Persian abodes,
And glittering temples of their hostile gods.
The princes applaud, with a furious joy;

And the king seiz'd a flambeau with zeal to destroy;
  Thais led the way,
  To light him to his prey,
And, like another Helen, fir'd another Troy.

    Thus, long ago,
  Ere heaving billows learn'd to blow,
    While organs yet were mute,
  Timotheus, to his breathing flute
    And sounding lyre,
Could swell the soul to rage, or kindle fierce desire.
  At last divine Cecilia came,
  Inventress of the vocal frame;
The sweet enthusiast, from her sacred store,
  Enlarg'd the former narrow bounds
  And added length to solemn sounds,
With nature's mother-wit, and arts unknown before.
  Let old Timotheus yield the prize,
    Or both divide the crown;
  He rais'd a mortal to the skies;
    She drew an Angel down.

ODE TO ST. CECILIA; 1698;

BY THOMAS BISHOP.

Set to Music by Daniel Purcell.

CECILIA, charming Saint! we raise
  Our souls to thee in songs of praise;
Fill with seraphic strains our thoughts,
With heav'nly music tune our notes:

For none dare speak or sing of thee
Unless inspir'd by sacred Harmony.

A tuneful concert then be made,
Bring in the lute and viol to our aid;
The joyful train of instruments command
    Taught by Cecilia's powerful hand.
See how the trembling strings all, at Cecilia's name,
In grateful notes give back their music whence it came;
    Behold how they rejoice to move,
And celebrate her once abode below, as now her reign
      above.

The melancholy flute forgets to mourn
    Forsaken Damon's sad despair;
    And all the rising notes return
    " Cecilia !" in a brisk and more exalted air.
    Tir'd with the rough alarms of war,
The martial trumpet hither does repair,
    Joys with a milder blast to swell,
    And on Cecilia's praises dwell;
    Joys here a peaceful Saint to yield
Those sounds due to the fighting hero and the noisy
      field.

    And the majestic organ, known
    Cecilia's care and art alone,
    That warms us with divine desires,
And kindles in our souls seraphic fires;
    The sounding organ does aspire
      With its monopoly

Of tuneful sounds to pierce the sky;
And join with its own Saint in concert in the heav'nly
    choir.

Cecilia's sacred memory,
   While Music lives, shall never die;
Music, the charming magnet of the whole,
   Of heav'n and earth the mighty soul!
   Music, that sweetens all our mirth,
   And gives new blooming joys their birth;
   That drives pale sorrow from our breast,
   And lulls our waking cares to rest;
   Our willing soul resigns to thee,
Thou tun'st its passions to thy harmony:
   By thee 'tis led at ev'ry turn,
   And even joys with thee to mourn;
Quick as its thoughts at ev'ry sound flies out,
And hovers o'er the trembling accent of each dying note.

To Music and Cecilia's name
Let ev'ry year return the same;
Whilst we the praise of both rehearse
In sounding accents, grateful verse;
And in those praises that we give,
We ourselves shall joyful live.

ODE FOR ST. CECILIA'S DAY, 1699.

BY THEOPHILUS PARSONS.

BLEST Cecilia! charming maid!
    Where shall mortals seek for aid
Thee to sing? Whose tuneful lays
Shall thy skill in music praise?
Inspir'd by thee, thy sons their duty show,
       And imitate below,
       With pious love
     What Angels sing above.
With breath the spacious organ fill;
With vital breath the trumpet swell;
Inspire the soft'ning flute with skill;
And let Cecilia, goddess of our song,
In melting accents ever dwell
On every string and every tongue.

For ever sacred be the day
Beyond all others bright and fair,
Ever joyous, ever gay,
When first divine Cecilia found
The magic art to quicken the long silent air
With all the energy of sound.
      Up to the skies
      On new-fledg'd wings,
From earth celestial music flies,
And joins in concert with the Cherubs' strings.
Down from their blissful bow'rs they came;

Came down to listen and admire
The mighty animated frame,
   Itself a quire.

   She smil'd,
Cecilia smil'd to see
   The Cherubs mild
With hov'ring wings descending from on high.
Like nimble lightning, swift and gay,
O'er all the keys her wanton fingers play;
The ready notes obey her touch:
   Dissolv'd in extacy
Th' immortal beings lie:
Divine Cecilia charms too much.

Her sprightly Treble, warbling sweet,
Glides through the veins
   On even feet,
And binds the soul in silken chains:
The yielding soul with softness it disarms,
And, like a woman, charms.

With manly grace the Bass stalks high,
Array'd in awful majesty:
Its haughty bound and pompous sound
The spirits warm, the soul alarm,
And shake the trembling air around.

Between the two extremes the Tenor flows
In gentle streams, persuading union as it goes.
And now in perfect harmony

The blended parts agree,
And glut the list'ning ear with melody.

   The Treble starts ;
On swift division leads the chace,
And quite outstrips the loit'ring parts.
The rumbling Bass with clumsy pace
Pursues the fleeting fugitive,
And all in triumph does her backward drive.
   But see !
The friendly Tenor, all for unity,
Does mildly interpose,
And joins them in a full compounded close.
   She paus'd awhile ;
For silence has in music place.
The ravish'd Cherubs, with a silent smile,
Disclose amazement on each face.
Again she plies the loud machine ;
Again entranc'd the Cherubs lie ;
Immortal, yet in pleasures almost die.
Thrice the lovely maid
Paus'd ; and thrice she play'd ;
And thrice she shew'd the pow'r divine
And wond'rous force of modulated sound,
That like a mighty torrent flows,
Victorious as it goes,
And sweeps away the strongest mound.

With breath the spacious organ fill ;
With vital breath the trumpet swell ;
Inspire the soft'ning flute with skill ;

And let Cecilia, goddess of our song,
In melting accents ever dwell
On every string and every tongue.

AN ODE FOR ST. CECILIA'S DAY, 1699 ;

BY JOSEPH ADDISON.

Set to Music by Daniel Purcell.

PREPARE the hallow'd strain, my muse,
  Thy softest sounds and sweetest numbers choose ;
The bright Cecilia's praise rehearse,
In warbling notes and gliding verse,
That smoothly run into a song,
And gently die away, and melt upon the tongue.

First let the sprightly violin
The joyful melody begin,
      And none of all her strings be mute,
While the sharp sound and shriller lay
In sweet harmonious notes decay,
      Soften'd and mellow'd by the flute.
" The flute that sweetly can complain,
Dissolve the frozen nymph's disdain,
Panting sympathy impart,
Till she partake her lover's smart."*

Now let the solemn organ join

---

* The last four lines of the second and third stanzas were
added by Nahum Tate.

Religious airs and strains divine
Such as may lift us to the skies,
And set all heaven before our eyes.
" Such as may lift us to the skies,
  So far at least till they
  Descend with kind surprise,
And meet our pious harmony half-way."

Let then the trumpet's piercing sound
Our ravish'd ears with pleasure wound ;
  The soul o'erpow'ring with delight ;
As, with a quick uncommon ray,
A streak of lightning clears the day,
  And flashes on the sight.
Let Echo too perform her part,
Prolonging every note with art,
  And in a low expiring strain
  Play all the concert o'er again.

Such were the tuneful notes that hung
On bright Cecilia's charming tongue :
Notes that sacred heats inspir'd
And with religious ardour fir'd :
The love-sick youth, that long supprest
His smother'd passion in his breast,
No sooner heard the warbling dame,
  But by the secret influence turn'd,
He felt a new diviner flame,
  And with devotion burn'd :
With ravish'd soul and looks amaz'd,
Upon her beauteous face he gaz'd ;

Nor made his amorous complaint:
In vain her eyes his heart had charm'd,
Her heavenly voice her eyes disarm'd,
    And chang'd the lover to a Saint.

And now the choir complete rejoices,
With trembling strings and melting voices,
    The tuneful ferment rises high
    And works with mingled melody:
Quick divisions run their rounds,
A thousand trills and quivering sounds
    In airy circles o'er us fly,
Till, wafted by a gentle breeze,
They faint and languish by degrees,
    And at a distance die.

ODE FOR ST. CECILIA'S DAY;

AUTHOR UNKNOWN.

Set to Music by Dr. Blow.

GREAT quire of heav'n, attend and bear a part,
We praise our heav'nly Patroness and art.
Be grave our lays, then sprightly; soft, then strong,
Like the great double subject of our song.

    Cecilia, great by nature's right,
    As Angels pious and as bright,
        Rais'd charming Music's fame;
    Music, by native right divine,

    Makes beauties with new glories shine
      And rais'd Cecilia's name.

    Cecilia did our art improve,
    Our art increas'd our sacred love ;
    The sweets of Music made her long
      To join in the seraphic song,
And her example drew the ravish'd throng.
    So when the trumpet sounds alarms,
    Britons, whom native valour warms,
Are double fir'd and fiercely run to arms.
To arms, to arms ! they cry, and all around,
Ten thousand braves return the welcome, warlike sound.

  Cecilia taught new graces to the quire,
  And made all instruments in one conspire.
By Music taught, in her harmonious mind
      All virtues in one concert join ;
      Faith, Hope, and Love the trebles were,
      Reason the tenor still was there,
        And, ev'ry part to grace,
        Humility the bass.

  While the Musician serv'd the Saint,
  What could she ask but Heav'n would grant ?
  When pray'rs on Music's wings arise,
  Heav'n, granting, does but sympathize.
  Let such a beauty sing and play,
  Angels themselves will run astray.
  None by such heav'nly beauty stray'd,
  'Twas heav'n where'er Cecilia play'd.

Music's best image was her face,
In ev'ry feature an harmonious grace
Disclaim'd the ear, and through the quicker sight
Inform'd the soul with fierce delight.
Nay Music's self in silent state was there,
There reign'd the peaceful softness of the flute ;
The melting, melting softness of the lute ;
The violins prevailing lively are,
Their melting, moving charms diffus'd around,
    Inimitable like her voice,
With something solemn like her organ's sound,
    At once to give and heal a wound,
        And, grieving, to rejoice.

      Hail, Music ! all our thoughts employ ;
      Love's food divine, life's purest joy,
      Blest speech of the celestial throng,
      Thou best and universal tongue,
Thou wing of zeal, and ev'ry passion's queen,
Thou spring, thou rule and soul of nature's grand ma-
      chine !

A HYMN TO HARMONY ;

WRITTEN IN HONOUR OF ST. CECILIA'S DAY,

1701;

BY WILLIAM CONGREVE.

Set to Music by John Eccles.

O HARMONY, to thee we sing,
   To thee the grateful tribute bring
Of sacred verse and sweet resounding lays ;

Thy aid invoking while thy pow'r we praise.
     All hail to thee
     All pow'rful Harmony!
Wise Nature owns thy undisputed sway,
Her wond'rous works resigning to thy care;
The planetary orbs thy rule obey,
And tuneful roll, unerring in their way,
Thy voice informing each melodious sphere.

Thy voice, O Harmony, with awful sound
     Could penetrate th' abyss profound,
     Explore the realms of ancient night,
And search the living source of unborn light.
     Confusion heard thy voice and fled,
And Chaos deeper plung'd his vanquish'd head.
     Then didst thou, Harmony, give birth
     To this fair form of heav'n and earth;
     Then all those shining worlds above
     In mystic dance began to move
Around the radiant sphere of central fire,
A never ceasing, never silent choir.

     Thou only, Goddess, first could'st tell
     The mighty charms in numbers found;
     And didst to heav'nly minds reveal
     The secret force of tuneful sound.
     When first Cyllenius form'd the lyre
       Thou didst the God inspire;
     When first the vocal shell he strung,
       To which the Muses sung:
Then first the Muses sung; melodious strains Apollo
     play'd,

And Music first began by thy auspicious aid.
    Hark, hark, again Urania sings !
Again Apollo strikes the trembling strings !
And see, the list'ning deities around,
Attend insatiate, and devour the sound.

        Descend, Urania, heav'nly fair,
    To the relief of this afflicted world repair ;
        See how with various woes opprest
        The wretched race of men is worn ;
        Consum'd with cares, with doubts distrest,
        Or by conflicting passions torn.
        Reason in vain employs her aid,
        The furious will on fancy waits ;
While reason still by hopes or fears betray'd,
Too late advances or too soon retreats.
Music alone with sudden charms can bind
The wand'ring sense, and calm the troubled mind.

Begin the pow'rful song, ye sacred Nine,
    Your instruments and voices join ;
    Harmony, peace, and sweet desire
        In ev'ry breast inspire.
Revive the melancholy drooping heart,
And soft repose to restless thoughts impart.
        Appease the wrathful mind
    To dire revenge and death inclin'd :
With balmy sounds his boiling blood assuage,
And melt to mild remorse his burning rage.
'Tis done ; and now tumultuous passions cease ;
    And all is hush'd, and all is peace.

The weary world with welcome ease is blest,
    By Music lull'd to pleasing rest.

    Ah, sweet repose, too soon expiring !
    Ah, foolish man, new toils requiring !
    Curs'd ambition, strife pursuing,
    Wakes the world to war and ruin.
    See, see, the battle is prepar'd ;
        Behold, the hero comes !
    Loud trumpets with shrill fifes are heard,
        And hoarse resounding drums.
    War with discordant notes and jarring noise,
        The harmony of peace destroys.

See the forsaken fair, with streaming eyes,
        Her parting lover mourn ;
    She weeps, she sighs, despairs, and dies,
And watchful, wastes the lonely livelong nights,
        Bewailing past delights
That may no more, no, never more return.
        O soothe her cares
        With softest sweetest airs,
    Till victory and peace restore
Her faithful lover to her tender breast,
    Within her folding arms to rest,
    Thence never to be parted more,
    No, never to be parted more.

    Enough, Urania, heav'nly fair,
    Now to thy native skies repair,
    And rule again the starry sphere ;

Cecilia comes, with holy rapture fill'd,
　　　To ease the world of care.
Cecilia, more than all the Muses skill'd !
　　　Phœbus himself to her must yield,
　　　And at her feet lay down
　　　His golden harp and laurel crown ;
The soft enervate lyre is drown'd
In the deep organ's more majestic sound.
In peals the swelling notes ascend the skies ;
Perpetual breath the swelling notes supplies,
　　　And lasting as her name
　　　Who form'd the tuneful frame,
　　　Th' immortal music never dies.

A SONG IN PRAISE OF ST. CECILIA.

Author unknown. Composed by Vaughan Richardson.

Y E tuneful and harmonious choir,
　　Who tend'rest thoughts and softest notes inspire,
Teach me in sweet melodious lays
To sing your mighty patroness's praise ;
Such moving notes, such tributary numbers bring,
As she, when here below, was wont herself to sing.

To thee, bright Saint, to thee we pay
The grateful honours of this day ;
Let ev'ry trumpet sound, and every viol play.

Let bright Cecilia's sacred name
On this blest day be Music's theme,
　　　For she is pleas'd o'er Music to preside ;

She made the disagreeing chords agree
In concord and uniting harmony,
 Music was her's and she was Music's pride.

To thee, bright Saint, to thee we owe
What we poor artists here below
Of Heav'n, of love and Music know.

ODE ON ST. CECILIA'S DAY.

Author unknown. Composed by George Holmes.

DOWN from the fix'd serene on high,
 Where all enjoy eternal rest;
Call'd by the powers of Harmony,
 Descend Cecilia to thy annual Feast.
See how thy votaries prepare
To smooth thy passage through the yielding air.
The charming and melodious flute
Would first her patroness salute;
In softest measures she delights to move,
And nothing breathes but gentlest airs of love.

All other music is by vocal crown'd,
 The voice o'er numbers bears the highest sway,
Gives a peculiar life to every sound,
And the most natural raptures does convey.
With voices then we'll fill the song,
 And thrice Cecilia call by name,
 Whilst echoing instruments repeat the same,
And strive to speak to make our chorus strong.

o

'Tis to joy most refin'd, and the chastest delight
That thus we presume our great Saint to incite,
With these she pass'd her happy days below,
Most like to them she does at present know.

Thus royal and triumphant Anna's mind
From Music does its chief refreshment find;
All other pleasures pall'd by empire's care,
Neglected by her, or untasted are.
Oh may the troubles which disturb the state,
Fast as her glorious conquests grow, abate;
May fears, and violence, and party cease,
And all conspire to court a common peace.

AN ODE IN PRAISE OF MUSIC, 1703.

BY JOHN HUGHES.

Set to Music by Philip Hart.

AWAKE, celestial Harmony!
    Awake, celestial Harmony!
Turn thy vocal sphere around,
Goddess of melodious sound.
Let the trumpet's shrill voice
And the drum's thund'ring noise
Rouse ev'ry dull mortal from sorrows profound.
    See, see,
  The mighty pow'r of Harmony!
Behold how soon its charms can chase
Grief and gloom from ev'ry face!

How swift its raptures fly,
And thrill through ev'ry soul, and brighten ev'ry eye.

Proceed, sweet charmer of the ear !
Proceed ; and through the mellow flute,
    The moving lyre,
    And solitary lute,
  Melting airs, soft joys inspire :
  Airs for drooping hope to hear,
  Melting as a lover's pray'r,
  Joys to flatter dull despair
And softly soothe the amorous fire.

  Now let the sprightly violin
    A louder strain begin ;
      And now
  Let the deep-mouth'd organ blow,
  Swell it high and sink it low.
    Hark ! how the treble and bass
  In wanton fugues each other chace,
And swift divisions run their airy race !
    Through all the travers'd scale they fly,
    In winding labyrinths of harmony ;
By turns they rise and fall, by turns we live and die.

Ye sons of art once more renew your strains ;
  In loftier verse and loftier lays
    Your voices raise
    To Music's praise !
  A nobler song remains.
  Sing how the Great Creator-God

On wings of flaming cherubs rode,
To make a world; and round the dark abyss
  Turn'd the golden compasses,*
The compasses in Fate's high store-house found;
  Thus far extend, He said, be this
    O world, thy measur'd bound.
Meanwhile a thousand harps were play'd on high;
    Be this thy measur'd bound,
    Was echo'd all around:
And now arise, ye earth and seas, and sky!
    A thousand voices made reply,
    Arise, ye earth and seas, and sky!

    What can Music's pow'r controul?
      When nature's sleeping soul
      Perceiv'd th' enchanted sound,
It wak'd and shook off foul deformity;
      The mighty melody
    Nature's secret chains unbound;
And earth arose, and seas, and sky.
      Aloft expanded spheres were slung
      With shining luminaries hung;
      A vast creation stood display'd,
      By Heav'n's inspiring Music made.
    O wondrous force of Harmony!

Divinest art, whose fame shall never cease!
Thy honour'd voice proclaim'd the Saviour's birth:
  When Heav'n vouchsaf'd to treat with earth,
  Music was herald of the peace:

---

* Milton.

Thy voice could best the joyful tidings tell;
 Immortal mercy! boundless love!
 A God descending from above
 To conquer Death and Hell.

 There yet remains an hour of fate,
When Music must again its charms employ.
 The trumpet's sound
Shall call the num'rous nations underground;
 The num'rous nations straight
Appear; and some with grief, and some with joy,
 Their final sentence wait.
 Then other arts shall pass away:
Proud Architecture shall in ruins lie,
 And Painting fade and die;
Nay earth, and heav'n itself, in wasteful fire decay.

 Music alone, and Poesy,
 Triumphant o'er the flame, shall see
 The world's last blaze.
 The tuneful sisters shall embrace,
 And praise and sing, and sing and praise
In never-ceasing choirs to all eternity.

ODE FOR ST. CECILIA'S DAY.

Author unknown.   Composed by Dr. Blow.

TRIUMPHANT Fame a thousand years
 Since Music did the globe inspire,
Divine Apollo equal to the spheres

Extoll'd, for wonders on his charming lyre:
Great god of wit and harmony still own'd,
His sacred brows with bays unfading crown'd,
And through the lofty sky in heav'n as earth renown'd.

Conquer'd Amphion homage paid,
    Arion, quell'd too, silent lies,
Orpheus, whom trees and rocks obey'd,
    All yielding him the prize.
'Till in succeeding time a wonder more renown'd
    Sprung from the noble organ's sound,
So sweetly finger'd by a lovely maid :
'Twas thought on earth some goddess play'd.

Close by a purling brook that ran
    Down through a shady cypress grove,
    Where, seeking his obdurate love,
Apollo wander'd all alone,
This wond'rous master-piece was done.
He pass'd when first the warbling echo came,
But soon each accent did his soul enflame,
So much the charmer charm'd ; Cecilia was her name.

Cecilia on the plains
Was empress of the swains,
    With roses round
    Her temples crown'd,
She plays and sings and reigns.
Attending too in concert join'd,
Were gather'd all the artful kind.
Now brisk violins they employ,

That fill ev'ry hearer with joy,
  And skilfully show
  With finger and bow,
  What mirth they can raise
  In hearts when they please,
And sorrow how quickly destroy.
A bolder, bolder touch inspiring,
Hearts with martial ardour firing,
A point of war and trumpets sounding,
Echoing notes aloud rebounding,
To battle move; and now they wound, they kill:
  A fierce alarm the drum does beat,
  Well-tim'd strokes with martial heat,
  Who, when the mingling sounds repeat,
    A noble chorus fill.

But now, ah now, a softer strain she plays,
(The lovely artist can all passions raise,)
Each melting note is love, and well does suit
The moving lyre and soul-delighting flute.
This charming air the amorous god gave pain;
He look'd and sigh'd, but look'd and sigh'd in vain,
He saw no yielding Daphne on the plain.
The varying notes then louder grew,
  And soon from love his thoughts to wonder raise,
Cecilia's art he admires anew;
Less than himself had envied too,
  Who now dissolves in praise;
Her's the precedence did confess
As music's queen and patroness,
  And crown'd her with his bays.

His heav'nly voice too then the god essay'd,
Apollo sung, divine Cecilia play'd;
The spheres in concert pow'rs divine employ,
And nature midst her labour felt a joy;
Perfection here in harmony was found,
Angels and list'ning Cherubs hover'd round,
Whilst universal praise exalts the more than mortal sound.

Join all then to sing
To Poetry's king,
And Music's fair queen.
The chorus begin.
So great is the theme
We're lost in extreme,
And only with joy
A wish can employ;
May arts be encourag'd with noblest endeavour,
May wit, love and harmony flourish for ever.

ODE FOR MUSIC ON ST. CECILIA'S DAY,
1708,
BY ALEXANDER POPE.

Set to Music about the year 1757 by William Walond.

DESCEND, ye Nine! descend and sing:
The breathing instruments inspire;
Wake into voice each silent string,
And sweep the sounding lyre!
In a sadly pleasing strain

Let the warbling lute complain :
    Let the loud trumpet sound,
    Till the roofs all around
    The shrill echoes rebound :
While in more lengthen'd notes and slow,
The deep, majestic, solemn organs blow.
    Hark ! the numbers soft and clear
    Gently steal upon the ear ;
    Now louder and yet louder rise,
    And fill with spreading sounds the skies ;
Exulting in triumph now swell the bold notes,
In broken air, trembling, the wild music floats ;
    Till, by degrees, remote and small,
      The strains decay
      And melt away
    In a dying, dying fall.

By Music, minds an equal temper know,
    Nor swell too high, nor sink too low ;
If in the breast tumultuous joys arise,
Music her soft, assuasive voice applies ;
    Or, when the soul is press'd with cares,
    Exalts her in enliv'ning airs :
Warriors she fires with animated sounds,
Pours balm into the bleeding lover's wounds ;
    Melancholy lifts her head,
    Morpheus rouses from his bed,
    Sloth unfolds her arms and wakes,
    List'ning Envy drops her snakes,
Intestine war no more our passions wage,
And giddy factions hear away their rage.

But when our country's cause provokes to arms,
How martial music ev'ry bosom warms!
So when the first bold vessel dar'd the seas,
High on the stern the Thracian rais'd his strain,
  While Argo saw her kindred trees
  Descend from Pelion to the main,
  Transported demigods stood round,
  And men grew heroes at the sound,
    Inflam'd with glory's charms:
Each chief his sev'nfold shield display'd,
And half unsheath'd the shining blade:
And seas, and rocks, and skies rebound
   To arms! to arms! to arms!

But when through all the infernal bounds,
Which flaming Phlegethon surrounds,
  Love, strong as Death, the Poet led
  To the pale nations of the dead,
What sounds were heard,
What scenes appear'd,
  O'er all the dreary coasts?
    Dreadful gleams,
    Dismal screams,
    Fires that glow,
    Shrieks of woe,
    Sullen moans,
    Hollow groans,
  And cries of tortur'd ghosts.
But hark! he strikes the golden lyre;
And see! the tortur'd ghosts respire,
  See, shady forms advance!

Thy stone, O Sisyphus, stands still,
Ixion rests upon his wheel,
   And the pale spectres dance!
The Furies sink upon their iron beds,
And snakes uncurl'd hang list'ning round their heads.
   By the streams that ever flow,
   By the fragrant winds that blow
     O'er the Elysian flow'rs;
   By those happy souls who dwell
   In yellow meads of asphodel,
     Or amaranthine bow'rs;
   By the heroes' armed shades,
   Glitt'ring through the gloomy glades;
   By the youths that died for love,
   Wand'ring in the myrtle grove;
Restore, restore Eurydice to life;
Oh take the husband, or return the wife!
   He sung, and Hell consented
     To hear the Poet's pray'r:
   Stern Proserpine relented,
     And gave him back the fair:
     Thus song could prevail
     O'er death and o'er Hell,
A conquest how hard and how glorious!
   Though Fate had fast bound her,
   With Styx nine times round her,
Yet Music and Love were victorious.

But soon, too soon, the lover turns his eyes:
Again she falls—again she dies—she dies!
How wilt thou now the fatal Sisters move?

No crime was thine if 'tis no crime to love.
  Now under hanging mountains,
  Beside the fall of fountains,
  Or where Hebrus wanders,
  Rolling in meanders,
        All alone,
    Unheard, unknown,
    He makes his moan :
    And calls her ghost,
  For ever, ever, ever lost !
  Now with Furies surrounded,
  Despairing, confounded,
  He trembles, he glows,
  Amidst Rhodope's snows :
See, wild as the winds, o'er the desert he flies ;
Hark ! Hæmus resounds with the Bacchanals' cries—
        Ah see, he dies !
Yet ev'n in death Eurydice he sung,
Eurydice still trembled on his tongue,
    Eurydice the woods,
    Eurydice the floods,
Eurydice the rocks and hollow mountains rung.

  Music the fiercest grief can charm,
  And fate's severest rage disarm ;
  Music can soften pain to ease,
  And make despair and madness please ;
  Our joys below it can improve,
  And antedate the bliss above.
  This the divine Cecilia found,
And to her Maker's praise confin'd the sound.

When the full organ joins the tuneful quire,
  Th' immortal pow'rs incline their ear:
Borne on the swelling notes our souls aspire,
While solemn airs improve the sacred fire;
  And Angels lean from Heav'n to hear.
Of Orpheus now no more let poets tell,
To bright Cecilia greater pow'r is giv'n;
  His numbers rais'd a shade from Hell,
  Hers lift the soul to Heav'n.

ALEXANDER'S FEAST, OR THE POWER
OF MUSIC.

AN ODE IN HONOUR OF ST. CECILIA'S DAY,

BY JOHN DRYDEN;

AS ALTERED IN THE YEAR 1711

BY JOHN HUGHES.

Set to Music by Thomas Clayton.

'TWAS at the royal feast, for Persia won
    By Philip's warlike son;
  Aloft in awful state
  The godlike hero sate
  On his imperial throne:
His valiant peers were plac'd around,
Their brows with roses and with myrtles bound.

  Lovely Thais by his side
  Blooming sat in beauty's pride.
  Happy, happy, happy pair!
None but the brave deserves the fair!

Timotheus plac'd on high,
Amid the tuneful quire,
With flying fingers touch'd the lyre;
Trembling the notes ascend the sky,
And heav'nly joys inspire.
The song began from Jove,
Who left his blissful seats above;
(Such is the pow'r of mighty love!)
A dragon's fiery form belied the god;
Sublime on radiant spires he rode,
When he to fair Olympia press'd,
And while he sought her snowy breast;
Then round her slender waist he curl'd,
And stamp'd an image of himself, a sov'reign of the world.
The list'ning crowd adore the lofty sound,
A present deity, they shout around;
A present deity, the echoing roofs rebound.

With ravish'd ears
The monarch hears,
Assumes the god,
Affects the nod,
And seems to shake the spheres.

The praise of Bacchus then the sweet musician sung,
Of Bacchus ever fair and ever young:
Behold he comes, the victor god!
Flush'd with a purple grace,
He shews his honest face;
As when, by tigers drawn, o'er India's plains he rode,
While loud with conquest and with wine,

His jolly troop around him reel'd along,
   And taught the vocal skies to join
      In this applauding song.

      Bacchus, ever gay and young,
      First did drinking joys ordain :
      Bacchus' blessings are a treasure ;
      Drinking is the soldier's pleasure ;
         Rich the treasure,
         Sweet the pleasure !
      Sweet is pleasure after pain !

Fir'd with the sound, the king grew vain ;
Fought all his battles o'er again,
And thrice he routed all his foes, and thrice he slew the
      slain.
   The master saw the madness rise,
   His glowing cheeks, his ardent eyes ;
   And while he heav'n and earth defy'd,
      He chose a mournful muse,
      Soft pity to infuse ;
Then thus he chang'd his song, and check'd his pride.

   See Darius great and good,
      By too severe a fate,
      Fallen from his high estate ;
   Behold his flowing blood !
   On earth th' expiring monarch lies,
   With not a friend to close his eyes.

With downcast looks the joyless victor sat,

Revolving in his alter'd soul,
The various turns of chance below ;
And, now and then, a sigh he stole,
    And tears began to flow.
The mighty master smil'd to see
That love was in the next degree :
'Twas but a kindred sound to move,
For pity melts the mind to love.
Softly sweet in Lydian measures,
Soon he sooth'd his soul to pleasures.

War is toil and trouble,
Honour is an airy bubble,
Never ending, still beginning,
Fighting still, and still destroying,
If the world be worth thy winning,
Think, O think it, worth enjoying :
Lovely Thais sits beside thee,
Take the good the gods provide thee.

The prince, unable to conceal his pain,
    Gaz'd on the fair
    Who caus'd his care,
And sigh'd and look'd, sigh'd and look'd,
Sigh'd and look'd, and sigh'd again :
At length, with love and wine at once oppress'd,
The vanquish'd victor sunk upon her breast.

Phœbus, patron of the lyre,
Cupid, god of soft desire,
How victorious are your charms !

Crown'd with conquest, full of glory,
See a monarch fall'n before ye,
Chain'd in beauty's clasping arms !

Now strike the golden lyre again ;
A louder yet, and yet a louder strain :
Break his bands of sleep asunder,
Rouse him, like a rattling peal of thunder.
Hark, hark, the horrid sound
Has rais'd up his head,
As awak'd from the dead,
And amaz'd he stares around.

Revenge, revenge, Alecto cries,
See the furies arise !
See the snakes that they rear,
How they hiss in their hair,
And the sparkles that flash from their eyes !

Behold a ghastly band,
Each a torch in his hand !
Those are Grecian ghosts, that in battle were slain,
And unburied remain,
Inglorious on the plain.
Give the vengeance due
To the valiant crew.
Behold how they toss their torches on high,
How they point to the Persian abodes,
And glitt'ring temples of their hostile gods !

The princes applaud with a furious joy ;

P

And the king seiz'd a flambeau, with zeal to destroy;
    Thais led the way,
    To light him to his prey,
  And, like another Helen, fir'd another Troy.

    Thus, long ago,
  Ere heaving bellows learn'd to blow,
    While organs yet were mute;
  Timotheus, to his breathing flute,
    And sounding lyre,
Could swell the soul to rage, or kindle soft desire.
    At last divine Cecilia came,
    Inventress of the vocal frame,
The sweet enthusiast, from her sacred store,
    Enlarg'd the former narrow bounds,
    And added length to solemn sounds,
With nature's mother-wit, and arts unknown before.

    Let old Timotheus yield the prize,
    Or both divide the crown;
    He rais'd a mortal to the skies,
    She drew an Angel down.

" SAUL DISPOSSESS'D :

AN ODE FOR ST. CECILIA'S DAY,

BY MR. J. B."

'TWAS at his house, in old Gabaa built,
  Sad Saul lay conscious of his guilt,
    With grace no longer bless'd,

Distracted, griev'd, oppress'd,
His brain disorder'd, and his soul possess'd.
See, see, he cries,
See the fiends where they rise!
Oh! help, they o'erpow'r me!
They snatch, they devour me!
Then wild from his couch all trembling he bounded,
In terror, in rage, and with phantoms confounded.
His friends around in anguish wait,
They weep, they wail, they mourn his fate;
In vain they mourn, they strive in vain
To calm his soul, and sooth his pain.
They heard of David's tuneful fame,
For him they sent, and David came.
He could to wonder touch the lyre,
Or gay or serious thoughts inspire;
Could soften pain and grief assuage,
Now lull the soul to soft desire,
Now rouse it into rage.

The Psalmist plac'd before the king,
Examin'd whence the madness came:
He soon betray'd the hateful spring,
And sought a proper theme.
Upon the harp his head reclin'd,
To that his ear intent was giv'n,
Cœlestial thoughts inflame his mind,
And now and then he stole an eye to heav'n.
First in gentle strains surprising,
Softly, sadly, sweetly rising,
Man, oh Man! why still pursuing,

Still he sung, thy own undoing!
Always falling, then repenting,
Wav'ring still, and still resolving,
Now rejoicing, then relenting,
Now in joys forbid dissolving.
Canst thou find, oh! find no measure,
Know no mean of pain or pleasure?
The notes prevail, kind soften'd thoughts impart,
Steal on the ear and sink into the heart.

Now David sings in numbers loud,
How Heav'n confounds th' unjust and proud,
Chastises those who doubt His sway,
And those who don't, and disobey.
He then began the fate of those
Who in the desert against Moses rose.
Behold while they their censers light,
And incense burn in his despite,
Corah, their chiefs, their goods and temples round,
At once down swallow'd in the gaping ground!
From Heav'n then pour'd a tempest of fire,
And in the flame the vulgar expire.
The king with terror hears,
Reflects, reviews his life;
He trembles, weeps, appears
All over thought and grief.

The Prophet soon perceiv'd the prince
Too sadly touch'd for his offence;
His sorrowing soul, o'ercome with fear
And grief, declining to despair.

Then sung in sprightly lays,
His sinking heart to raise:
Man is the darling of the sky,
God views us with a parent's eye;
For Heaven He designs us,
From error reclines us;
And while His commands we obey,
We gain ourselves treasures
Of joys and of pleasures,
Of pleasures that never decay.
And though greatly and often we stray,
If pardon repentant we pray,
With joy He gives ear,
With grace crowns our pray'r,
Why should we, why should we, why should we,
Why should we then ever despair?
All over the skies
Hosannas arise,
And Heav'n is declar'd forgiving and wise.
Reviv'd at the sound
The prince star'd around,
He breath'd, and he hop'd, and comfort he found.

But lo! the wicked fiend within
Would fain pervert his hope to sin,
And to presumption swell his soul again.
Who'd lead a painful life,
When sighs, a moment's grief,
Regain departed grace,
And blackest crimes efface?
This the divine exorcist hears,

The pleasing medicine soon prepares;
Kindly checks in feeling measures,
All his love, his bent to pleasures.

Oh Gideon! Gideon! once so great,
    So dreadful in the listed plain,
Now where is all the regal state,
    How short-liv'd all thy pompous reign!
The great, the just, the glorious, brave,
Like Madian fills the silent grave:
Thousands no more confess his sway,
    In dust he lies, a reptile's prey.
A doleful murmur fills the vaulted room,
While, each reflecting on his future doom,
Saul checks his pride, and ceases to presume.
    Prostrate he falls, reveres the skies,
        With pray'rs propitiates Heav'n,
    With lifted hands and flowing eyes
        Implores to be forgiv'n.

    But hark! how nobler strains surprise!
Spreading and loud the solemn notes arise,
And in exalted sounds slow, length'ning, mount the skies.
    O Lord of Hosts! how bless'd are they
    Who act obsequious to Thy sway!
    Thy arm the wicked lays in dust,
    Thy arm exalts and shields the just:
    Thy nod can shake the mighty ball;
    Before Thy thunder armies fall;
From Thee all good, all life descend,
        And Thou art all in all;

Sole Lord of heav'n and earth and hell,
Unfelt, unheard, invisible;
Too vast for mortal tongue to tell,
　Or thought to comprehend.
With love and fear of Heav'n inspir'd,
Saul stood in raptures, and admir'd
　The Psalmist's bless'd harmonious art.
No more to rage or grief inclin'd,
Prospects divine engage his mind,
　And gladness fills his heart.
Thus David's harp could mend the soul,
The black attempts of hell controul;
　And Music thus, in former days,
　Resounded sweet th' Almighty's praise,
Could calm the mind to peace, and heav'nly raptures
　　　raise.
　In after times its force decays,
　To soften'd sounds confin'd,
　Poorly content the ear to please,
　　But not exalt the mind.
Divine Cecilia came at length,
Improv'd its sweetness, and reviv'd its strength,
Her Author's praise harmoniously renew'd,
And David's bold cœlestial strains pursu'd.
　When the loud nervous organ sounds,
　We hear, we hear we know not what,
　Something solemn, something great,
　　Wrapt in the skies, ourselves no more,
　　Scorn earthly things we sought before,
　And fir'd with more than mortal heat,
　　Contemn all narrow bounds.

Swell all ye organs, inspire ev'ry flute !
Leave, heav'nly minstrels, no instrument mute !
Revive ev'ry lyre, awake ev'ry string,
And loudly resound the Virgin and King !
 He could a prince's rage appease,
  A wicked fiend disarm ;
 She could to heav'n an atheist raise,
  And did an Angel charm.

ODE FOR MUSIC ;

BY ALEXANDER POPE :

BEING AN ALTERATION, MADE IN THE YEAR 1730, OF HIS
ODE FOR ST. CECILIA'S DAY, 1708.

Set to Music by Dr. Maurice Greene.

DESCEND, ye Nine ! descend and sing ;
 The breathing instruments inspire ;
Wake into voice each silent string,
And sweep the sounding lyre !
 In a sadly pleasing strain
 Let the warbling lute complain :
In more lengthen'd notes and slow,
The deep, majestic solemn organs blow.
 Hark ! the numbers soft and clear,
 Gently steal upon the ear ;
  Now louder they sound,
  Till the roofs all around
  The shrill echoes rebound :
 Till, by degrees, remote and small,

The strains decay,
And melt away
In a dying, dying fall.

By music minds an equal temper know,
Nor swell too high, nor sink too low.
If in the breast tumultuous joys arise,
Music her soft, assuasive voice applies ;
Or when the soul is sunk in cares,
Exalts her with enliv'ning airs.
Warriors she fires with sprightly sounds ;
Pours balm into the lover's wounds :
Passions no more the soul engage,
Ev'n factions hear away their rage.

Amphion thus bade wild dissension cease,
And soften'd mortals learn'd the arts of peace.
Amphion taught contending kings
From various discords to create
The music of a well-tun'd state,
Nor slack nor strain the tender strings ;
Those usual touches to impart
That strike the subject's answ'ring heart ;
And the soft silent harmony that springs
From sacred union and consent of things.

But when our country's cause provokes to arms,
How martial music ev'ry bosom warms !
When the first vessel dar'd the seas
The Thracian rais'd his strain,
And Argo saw her kindred trees

Descend from Pelion to the main.
Transported demigods stood round,
And men grew heroes at the sound,
    Inflam'd with glory's charms !
Each chief his sev'nfold shield display'd,
And half unsheath'd the shining blade :
And seas, and rocks, and skies rebound
    To arms, to arms, to arms !

But when through all the infernal bounds
Which flaming Phlegethon surrounds,
    Sad Orpheus sought his consort lost ;
      The adamantine gates were barr'd,
      And nought was seen and nought was heard
    Around the dreary coast,
      But dreadful gleams,
      Dismal screams,
      Fires that glow,
      Shrieks of woe,
      Sullen moans,
      Hollow groans,
And cries of tortur'd ghosts !
But hark ! he strikes the golden lyre ;
And see ! the tortur'd ghosts respire !
    See, shady forms advance !
    And the pale spectres dance !
The Furies sink upon their iron beds,
And snakes uncurl'd hang list'ning round their heads.

    By the streams that ever flow,
    By the fragrant winds that blow

O'er th' Elysian flow'rs ;
By those happy souls that dwell
In yellow meads of asphodel,
Or amaranthine bow'rs :
By the heroes' armed shades
Glitt'ring through the gloomy glades,
By the youths that died for love,
Wand'ring in the myrtle grove ;
Restore, restore Eurydice to life,
Oh take the husband or return the wife !

He sang, and hell consented
To hear the poet's pray'r ;
Stern Proserpine relented,
And gave him back the fair.
Thus song could prevail
O'er death and o'er hell :
A conquest how hard and how glorious !
Though fate had fast bound her
With Styx nine times round her,
Yet Music and Love were victorious.

ODE FOR ST. CECILIA'S DAY ;

BY THE REV. MR. VIDAL.

Set to Music by William Boyce.

THE charms of Harmony display
Of Heaven's Omnipotence a ray :
Sov'reign queen o'er human souls,
Each care, each passion she controuls ;

On earth she ev'ry pow'r can quell,
And bring departed ghosts from hell.

If the hopeless lover's heart
   Sinks down, oppress'd with woe ;
Dead'ned by the bleeding smart,
   The stream of life runs low.
Music's healing voice applied,
   He hears away his pain ;
Gently swells the spirit's tide,
   Then briskly springs again.

Where peace prevails and plenty flows,
   These blessings Harmony ensures,
Heightens the joy which peace bestows,
   From plenty new delight procures.
       In war's fierce alarms
       The bravest she warms.
       By Music elate,
         Nor fearing to die,
       Though doubtful's their fate,
         To battle they fly.
    When the trumpet loudly calls
    To arms, all terror falls ;
    Rous'd up, ev'n cowards boast,
    Their fright in courage lost.

Yet is not melody confin'd
To soothe the breasts of human kind :
Her piercing sounds can quickly wing
Their flight to the Almighty King.

Cecilia sings and strikes the lyre ;
Her melting notes with raptures fire ;
Heav'n's gates fly open at her plaint,
And raise the Woman to a Saint.

ODE FOR ST. CECILIA'S DAY,

BY JOHN LOCKMAN.

Set to Music by William Boyce.

SEE fam'd Apollo and the Nine
   On Pindus' flow'ry hill !
Their notes that in loud concert join,
   The winding vallies fill :
Th' assembled Deities all their art display ;
Love, the great theme of their united lay.

   Immortal Love, with tuneful lyres
     Lo ! the song to thee we raise ;
   Thou, who ev'ry breast inspires,
     Thus to warble forth thy praise.
   Thy blessings, which for ever flow,
     Speak thee gracious and divine.
   Enchanting Power ! to thee we owe
     Worlds on worlds that round us shine.

Aloft the strains melodious swiftly fly,
The æther pierce, and reach the inmost sky :
The clouds divide, the Gods appear around ;
Silent they bend, attracted by the sound.

When a tender, virtuous passion
    Mutually two lovers feel,
When their secret inclination
    Sighing they in words reveal:
        Thus to languish
        Free from anguish,
    O what transports they enjoy!
        These are treasures,
        These are pleasures,
Charm the soul and never cloy.

Hark! the loud trumpet calls a youth to arms;
By glory rous'd, he pants for war's alarms.
In vain his nymph's fond tears would tempt his stay;
He breathes a sigh, then tears himself away.

    The hero whom a fair one fires,
        Untaught to yield,
        Hastes to the field:
        'Midst fiercest foes
        Intrepid goes;
    He charges, and the host retires.
Whilst round he whirls his fatal spear,
    The drum's hoarse voice, the cannon's roar,
Are glorious music to his ear;
    For soon the foe will life implore.

Ah! say, could Painting, could the weeping Muse,
Soft moving words, or gloomy colours choose,
Tho' the twin arts had all their pow'rs combin'd,
To draw a dying lover's tortur'd mind.

What cruel pangs the lover feels,
  Who soon must bid adieu
To her whose face a heav'n reveals,
  Which he no more must view!
But doom'd to wander, lost, forlorn,
  In myrtle shades below:
Doom'd his own fate, his nymph's, to mourn,
  And nourish endless woe.

Thus, whilst the Muse Love's boundless influence sings,
The Gods applaud, and all Olympus rings.

  Sprung from Gods, immortal Love
    O'er the mind triumphant reigns:
  Wond'rous Pow'r! by thee we prove
    Bitter sweets and pleasing pains.

  Hail Harmony! amazing source
    Of blessings Gods and men enjoy;
  Inspir'd, we sing thy awful course,
    Which ceasing would the world destroy.
  Till thou cam'st forth all nature lay
    Dark as the abyss profound:
  But at thy gloom-dispelling ray,
    Enchanting glories darted round.
  Gracious Power, to thee we owe
    Music, daughter of the sky:
  Softest spell to lighten woe,
    Strongest charm to heighten joy.

At Music's sacred name, a blaze of light
Streams round the globe, and instant takes from sight

The list'ning Deities, the Muses' hill;
Hush'd are the sounds and the whole æther still.

With celestial glory crown'd,
(Awful Saints exulting round)
See Cecilia slow descend,
And to earth her progress bend!
Their bright charge, through fields of air,
Angels on their pinions bear:
Waft her harp along the sky,
And, enchanted, round her fly.

Mortals, in hymns of tuneful joy,
   Her presence greet, her virtues praise;
Their noblest instruments employ,
   And, as to heav'n, their voices raise.

In solemn chorus now they join,
   And now distinct they sound,
On hautboys, warbling flutes refine,
   And spread enchantment round.

Gently each breast gay viols warm,
   And wake a fond desire,
With lofty accents trumpets charm,
   And mighty thoughts inspire.

The trebles raise, the basses sink
   By turns the ravish'd soul;
Strange magic at the ear to drink,
   Sounds that each pulse controul!

Music, gently soothing Power,
In what cloud-surrounded bower,
Far removed, in deep disguise,
Dost thou hide from human eyes?
What art thou, sweet being, say,
When thou warblest from the spray;
When thou wak'st the sleeping string;
What art thou when Angels sing?

Pleas'd the celestial visitant surveys
Mankind, thus celebrating Music's praise.
Swift o'er her face seraphic glories play,
Whose splendours emulate the solar ray:
Cherubs around the sacred minstrel throng,
Whilst mortals thus pursue the joyful song.

As nature with the sun revives,
    The magnet kindred iron draws,
As cold with heat incessant strives,
    Each orb obeys the gen'ral laws:
So sounds harmonious, soft or strong,
    Airy or grave, or sharp or sweet,
The passions fondly draw along,
    Whilst, round each heart, the accents beat.

The captive, bound in rankling chains,
Who sadly of his fate complains,
If Music speaks, no anguish knows,
But, sweetly lull'd, forgets his woes.
Her voice can charm the fiercest grief,
And o'er the mind breathe soft relief.

The melting theme transports each mortal breast,
Wakes ev'ry joy and gives to sorrow rest !
And whilst the strains the softest thoughts inspire,
A voice proceeds, and lifts the subject higher.

> Music can the passions raise,
>   Wake the soul with sweet surprise,
> Swiftly as the lightning's blaze,
>   O'er the earth, wide-spreading, flies.

Now the ætherial lyrist sweeps the strings,
And thus, responsive to her harp, she sings.

> Mortals, scorn the boasted Nine,
> Sing of Love, but Love Divine,
>   Vain are all terrestrial things.
> They, or soon or late, decay,
> Flourish now, now glide away,
>   Blades of grass and thrones of kings.

> Leave transient joys, and raise the theme
>   To glories which enchant the eye ;
> Where endless sunshine, bliss supreme,
>   Encircle those who wing the sky.
> Display His goodness, Hail His might,
> Who nature call'd from boundless night,
> And pour'd o'er all a flood of light.
> Thus will your hymns, like incense, rise
> To heav'n, a grateful sacrifice,
> And draw new blessings from the skies.

ODE ON ST. CECILIA'S DAY,

BY CHRISTOPHER SMART.

Set to Music, about the year 1800, *by William Russell.*

FROM your lyre-enchanted towers,
    Ye musically mystic Powers,
Ye that inform the tuneful spheres,
Inaudible to mortal ears,
While each orb in ether swims
Accordant to th' inspiring hymns ;
Hither Paradise remove,
Spirits of harmony and love !
Thou too, divine Urania, deign to appear,
    And with thy sweetly-solemn lute
    To the grand argument the numbers suit ;
        Such as sublime and clear,
        Replete with heavenly love,
    Charm th' inraptur'd souls above.
    Disdainful of fantastic play,
        Mix on your ambrosial tongue
        Weight of sense with sound of song,
    And be angelically gay.

And you, ye sons of Harmony below,
    How little less than Angels when ye sing !
With emulation's kindling warmth shall glow,
    And from your mellow modulating throats
    The tribute of your grateful notes
In union of piety shall bring.

Shall Echo from her vocal cave
Repay each note the shepherd gave,
And shall we not our mistress praise,
And give her back the borrow'd lays?
But further still our praises we pursue;
  For ev'n Cecilia, mighty maid,
  Confess'd she had superior aid—
She did—and other rites to greater Powers are due.
 Higher swell the sounds and higher:
  Let the winged numbers climb:
 To the heaven of heavens aspire,
  Solemn, sacred and sublime:
 From heaven Music took its rise;
 Return it to its native skies.

 Music's a celestial art;
  Cease to wonder at its power,
 Though lifeless rocks to motion start,
  Though trees dance lightly from the bower,
 Though rolling floods in sweet suspense
 Are held, and listen into sense.
In Penshurst's plains, when Waller, sick with love,
Has found some silent solitary grove,
Where the vague moonbeams pour a silver flood
Of tremulous light athwart th' unshaven wood,
  Within an hoary, moss-grown cell,
He lays his careless limbs without reserve,
And strikes, impetuous strikes each querulous nerve
   Of his resounding shell.
 In all the woods, in all the plains
 Around a lively stillness reigns:

The deer approach the secret scene,
And weave their way through labyrinths green ;
While Philomela learns the lay,
And answers from the neighbouring bay.
    But Medway, melancholy mute,
      Gently on his urn reclines,
    And all-attentive to the lute,
      In uncomplaining anguish pines :
    The crystal waters weep away,
    And bear the tidings to the sea :
      Neptune in the boisterous seas
    Spreads the placid bed of peace,
        While each blast,
        Or breathes it last,
Or just does sigh a symphony and cease.

Behold Arion—on the stern he stands,
    Pall'd in theatrical attire,
To the mute strings he moves th' enlivening hands,
    Great in distress, and wakes the golden lyre :
While in a tender Orthian strain
He thus accosts the mistress of the main :
    By the bright beams of Cynthia's eyes,
    Through which your waves attracted rise,
      And actuate the hoary deep ;
      By the secret coral cell,
    Where Love and Joy and Neptune dwell,
      And peaceful floods in silence sleep ;
    By the sea-flowers that immerge
    Their heads around the grotto's verge,
      Dependent from the stooping stem ;

By each roof-suspended drop,
That lightly lingers on the top,
    And hesitates into a gem ;
By thy kindred watery gods,
The lakes, the rivulets, founts and floods,
And all the powers that live unseen
Underneath the liquid green ;
  Great Amphitrite, (for thou canst bind
  The storm and regulate the wind,)
Hence waft me, fair goddess, oh ! waft me away,
Secure from the men, and the monsters of prey.

He sung—The winds are charm'd to sleep,
Soft stillness steals along the deep,
The Tritons and the Nereids sigh
In soul-reflecting sympathy,
And the whole audience of waters weep.
But Amphitrite her dolphin sends—the same
Which erst to Neptune brought the nobly-perjur'd dame.
  Pleas'd to obey the beauteous monster flies,
And on his scales as the gilt sunbeams play,
    Ten thousand variegated dies
    In copious streams of lustre rise,
Rise o'er the level main and signify his way.
  And now the joyous bard, in triumph bore,
Rides the voluminous wave, and makes the wish'd-for
        shore.
      Come, ye festive social throng,
      Who sweep the lyre, or pour the song,
      Your noblest melody employ,
      Such as becomes the mouth of joy ;

Bring the sky-aspiring thought,
With bright expression richly wrought;
And hail the Muse ascending on her throne,
The main at length subdued, and all the world her own.

But o'er the affections too she claims the sway,
Pierces the human heart, and steals the soul away;
And as attractive sounds move high or low,
Th' obedient ductile passions ebb and flow.
Has any nymph her faithful lover lost,
And in the visions of the night,
And all the day-dreams of the light,
In sorrow's tempest turbulently tost—
From her cheek the roses die,
The radiations vanish from her sun-bright eye,
And her breast, the throne of love,
Can hardly, hardly, hardly move,
To send th' ambrosial sigh.
But let the skilful bard appear,
And pour the sounds medicinal in her ear:
Sing some sad, some plaintive ditty,
Steep'd in tears that endless flow,
Melancholy notes of pity,
Notes that mean a world of woe;
She too shall sympathize, she too shall moan,
And pitying others' sorrows sigh away her own.

Wake, wake the kettle-drum, prolong
The swelling trumpet's silver song,
And let the kindred accents pass
Through the horn's meandering brass.

Arise—The patriot Muse invites to war,
   And mounts Bellona's brazen car;
   While Harmony, terrific maid!
   Appears in martial pomp array'd:
   The sword, the target, and the lance
She wields, and, as she moves, exalts the Pyrrhic dance.
   Trembles the earth, resounds the skies—
   Swift o'er the fleet, the camp she flies,
With thunder in her voice, and lightning in her eyes.
   The gallant warriors engage
   With inextinguishable rage
     And hearts unchill'd with fear;
   Fame numbers all the chosen bands,
   Full in the front fair Victory stands,
     And Triumph crowns the rear.

But hark! the temple's hollow'd roof resounds,
And Purcell lives along the solemn sounds.—
   Mellifluous, yet manly too,
     He pours his strains along,
   As from the lion Samson slew,
     Comes sweetness from the strong.
   Not like the soft Italian swains,
   He trills the weak enervate strains,
     Where sense and music are at strife;
   His vigorous notes with meaning teem,
   With fire, with force explain the theme,
     And sing the subject into life.
Attend—he sings Cecilia—matchless dame!
'Tis she, 'tis she,—fond to extend her fame,
On the loud chords the notes conspire to stay,

And sweetly swell into a long delay,
   And dwell delighted on her name.

     Blow on, ye sacred organs, blow,
     In tones magnificently slow;
     Such is the music, such the lays
     Which suit your fair inventress' praise:
     While round religious silence reigns,
     And loitering winds expect the strains.
     Hail majestic mournful measure,
     Source of many a pensive pleasure!
     Blest pledge of love to mortals given,
     As pattern of the rest in heaven!
     And thou, chief honour of the veil,
     Hail, harmonious virgin, hail!
When Death shall blot out every name,
And Time shall break the trump of Fame,
     Angels may listen to thy lute:
Thy power shall last, thy bays shall bloom,
When tongues shall cease, and worlds consume,
     And all the tuneful spheres be mute.

A BURLESQUE ODE ON ST. CECILIA'S DAY.

BY BONNELL THORNTON.

Set to Music by Dr. Charles Burney.

B E dumb, be dumb, ye inharmonious sounds,
   And Music that th' astonish'd ear with discord
      wounds :
No more let vulgar rhymes profane the day,
   Grac'd with divine Cecilia's name ;
Let solemn hymns this awful feast proclaim,
And heav'nly notes conspire to raise the heav'nly lay.
      The viler melody we scorn,
         Which meaner instruments afford ;
      Shrill flute, sharp fiddle, bellowing horn,
   Rumbling bassoon, or tinkling harpsichord.
In strains more exalted the salt-box shall join,
And clattering, and battering, and clapping combine ;
With a rap and a tap while the hollow side sounds,
Up and down leaps the flap, and with rattling rebounds.
      Strike, strike the soft Judaic harp,
   By teeth coercive in firm durance kept,
   And lightly by the volant finger swept.
         Buzzing twangs the iron lyre,
            Shrilly, thrilling,
            Trembling, trilling,
         Whizzing with the wav'ring wire.

      Hark, how the banging marrow-bones
      Make clanging cleavers ring,

With a ding dong, ding dong,
 Ding dong, ding dong,
Ding dong, ding dong, ding dong, ding.
Raise your uplifted arms on high ;
 In loud prolonged tones
  Let cleavers sound
  A merry merry round
 By banging marrow bones.

Cease, lighter numbers : hither bring
 The undulating string
Stretch'd out, and to the tumid bladder
 In amity harmonious bound ;
Then deeper swell the notes and sadder,
And let the hoarse bass slowly solemn sound.
 With dead, dull, doleful heavy hums,
  With dismal moans,
  And mournful groans,
 The sober hurdy-gurdy thrums.
With magic sounds like these did Orpheus' lyre
 Motion, sense, and life inspire ;
 When, as he play'd, the list'ning flood
Still'd its loquacious waves, and silent stood ;
The trees swift bounding danc'd with loosen'd stumps,
And sluggish stones caper'd in active jumps.
  Each ruddy breasted robin
  The concert bore a bob in,
 And ev'ry hooting owl around ;
   The croaking frogs,
   The grunting hogs,
 All, all conspire to join the echoing sound.

Now to Cecilia, heav'nly maid,
    Your loud united voices raise :
With solemn joy to celebrate her praise
    Each instrument shall lend its aid.
The salt-box with clattering and clapping shall sound,
        The iron lyre
    Buzzing twang with wav'ring wire,
        With heavy hum
    The hurdy-gurdy sadly thrum,
And the merry merry marrow-bones ring round.
    Such matchless strains Cecilia knew,
    When Angels from their heav'nly sphere
    By Harmony's strong pow'r she drew,
Whilst ev'ry Spirit above would gladly stoop to hear.

THE END.

CHISWICK PRESS :
C. WHITTINGHAM, TOOKS COURT, CHANCERY LANE.

For EU product safety concerns, contact us at Calle de José Abascal, 56–1°,
28003 Madrid, Spain or eugpsr@cambridge.org.

www.ingramcontent.com/pod-product-compliance
Ingram Content Group UK Ltd.
Pitfield, Milton Keynes, MK11 3LW, UK
UKHW040616240426
470322UK00010B/160